PROPHET OF ISLAM
AND
HIS TEACHINGS

other recent reference works from cosmo publications . . .

REDISCOVERING ISLAM.
ENCYCLOPAEDIA OF ISLAMIC STUDIES
in 35 volumes

ENCYCLOPAEDIA OF ISLAMIC MYSTICISM AND SUFISM
in 23 volumes

INTERNATIONAL ENCYCLOPAEDIA OF ISLAMIC HISTORY
in 12 volumes

INTERNATIONAL ENCYCLOPAEDIA OF
GREAT ISLAMIC DYNASTIES
in 4 volumes

THE MUSLIMS.
ENCYCLOPAEDIA OF ISLAM
in 11 volumes

BIOGRAPHICAL ENCYCLOPAEDIA OF ISLAM
in 4 volumes
Edited by M Th Houstma et al

DICTIONARY OF ISLAM
Patrick Hughes
in 2 volumes

ENCYCLOPAEDIA OF ISLAMIC PHILOSOPHY
in 12 volumes

ENCYCLOPAEDIA OF ISLAMIC SCIENTISTS AND SCHOLARS
in 5 volumes

For getting information on our forthcoming books please write to us.

PROPHET OF ISLAM
AND
HIS TEACHINGS

By

MAULVI ABDUL KARIM, B.A., M.L.C.

President, Muhammadan Educational Conference, Bengal; Honorary Fellow of the University of Calcutta; President, Bengal Presidency Muslim League; Inspector of Schools, Bengal; Member, Bengal Legislative Council.

Second Edition

Cosmo Publications

2011 **INDIA**

PROPHET OF ISLAM AND HIS TEACHINGS

First Published by
Cosmo Publications, 2011

ISBN 978-81-307-1244-4

Published by
COSMO PUBLICATIONS
24-B, Ansari Road, Darya Ganj,
New Delhi-110 002, INDIA
email.: genesis@ndb.vsnl.net.in
cosmopublications@gmail.com

Printed and Bound in India

A VIEW OF PROPHET'S TOMB AT MEDINA

PREFACE

The more we study Islam the more are we convinced that this religion of which universalism is the most distinctive feature, all-round progress the main key-note, and the unity of God and equality of man the chief message, is intended for the whole of mankind. Another unique feature of Islam is that it is antagonistic to no true religion and acknowledges and reveres the prophets of all great religions and invites all peoples to the path of purity and virtuous life.

If there is any religion that can effectively withstand the atheism, agnosticism and materialism that are gradually getting a hold over the entire civilised world, it is Islam, which has harmonised every progress made by philosophy and science. If it is taken into consideration what the Arabs were before the Prophet's advent and what they became after it, this conclusion cannot be avoided.

The progress Islam has already made, while still in its fourteenth century, is beyond the wildest dream of its early propagators. It has spread over the whole continent of Africa and a very large part of Asia. A movement is on foot to Islamize Europe and America. England has made a rather ready response to the call of Islam ; hundreds of Englishmen and women of all ranks and positions have already embraced Islam. In such circumstances it may not be unreasonable to expect that, before long, Islam will spread from one end of the world to the other, establishing peace and good-will on earth and binding all the races and communities all over the globe into one common fraternity. The dynamic effect of the all-round progress that is being made by the rejuvenated and modernised Islamic countries like Turkey, Persia, Afghanistan, Hedjaz, and Egpyt, must inevitably expedite this happy consummation.

In this work an endeavour has been made to refute the false imputations made against Hazrat Muhammad by prejudiced critics and to prove that he was a true Messenger of God and one of the greatest reformers and benefactors of mankind. Misrepresentation of facts and misinterpretation of motives by non-Muslims may not be unnatural ; but what is very regrettable is that some of the present-day educated Muslims should have failed to form a correct estimate of the life and teachings of their own Prophet. This is perhaps the result of scepticism and materialistic ideas engendered by godless occidental education.

In conclusion, the author gratefully acknowledges the invaluable assistance he received from the works of some Muslim and non-Muslim writers on the subject, availing himself even of their language in some places where he thought it unfair to try to improve on their beautiful and expressive language. It has not been possible to indicate this fact in some cases and so a general acknowledgment is frankly made here. The author's thanks are due also to Professor Abdur Rahim, M.A., for looking through the draft and correcting errors that had crept into the proof sheets.

Calcutta, 15th January, 1936. The Author.

PREFACE TO THE SECOND EDITION

The first edition of the "Prophet of Islam and His Teachings," which has been prescribed as a text-book for Classes VII and VIII, has been exhausted. A revised edition of the book, which has been translated at Cochin into Malayalam, is, therefore published.

The Author.

1-3-37.

*

CONTENTS

*

*

PROPHET OF ISLAM

AND

HIS TEACHINGS

INTRODUCTION

It is a historical fact that when mankind swayed by passions became engrossed in the gratification of their carnal desires and went stray from the path of virtue and righteousness, God was pleased to send some inspired persons to purify the demoralised people by teaching them moral and religious truths and by pointing out to them the errors into which they had fallen. The advent of these Messengers was at each stage in accordance with the needs of the times and the requirements of the people. All of them played their part well in the reclamation and regeneration of the human race.

When such a Messenger made his appearance, some people exalted him to godhead by investing him with divine attributes, while others denounced him as a mere impostor. That neither of these outlooks was correct needs no arguments. For, respect and reverence are due to all the Messengers of God and it is nothing but impudence on the part of man either to exaggerate or to underrate their attributes bestowed by God for the spiritual evolution of His creatures.

Fourteen hundred years ago when there was spiritual stagnation all over the world, when gross immorality and rank superstition swayed all mankind, and when horrible religious persecution and disgraceful wrangling over creeds played havoc with the social harmony and political homogenity of the human race, God out of His mercy sent a Messenger to warn His creatures and to call them to the right path.

The advent of such a Messenger was not unanticipated at the time, foreshadowed as it had been by some of the Messengers, whom the Lord had sent before from time to time for the reclamation of debased humanity. This was the Holy Prophet of Arabia, whose greatness has not, to my mind, yet been rightly appraised by mankind nor have his inestimable services to humanity been universally recognised and adequately appreciated. It is indeed difficult to form a correct and just estimate of his true personality either from the fanciful descriptions of his over-zealous panegyrists or from the malicious denunciations of his narrow-minded detractors. The real Muhammad (upon whom be peace) is hidden under the exaggerated adulation on the one hand and unjustifiable calumniation on the other. Cleared of the panegyrics and calumnies heaped upon him, Hazrat Muhammad emerges as one of the noblest characters human history has ever produced and the greatest benefactor mankind has ever been blessed with. "And we have not sent thee except as a blessing unto the universe". Al-Quran.

---

*

*

CHAPTER I

LIFE OF HAZRAT MUHAMMAD

Childhood

On the 29th August 570 A.D., there was born at Mecca, in a highly respectable Quraish family, a child destined to inaugurate a mighty movement, spiritual, moral, intellectual, social and political; perhaps the mightiest history has recorded—a movement that, in the words of Gibbon, "impressed a lasting character on the nations of the globe". This child was named Muhammad, the praised one. His father, Abdullah, had died before his birth and he lost his mother, Amina, when he was barely six years old. He then came under the protection of his grandfather, Abdul Muttalib, who passed away before the orphan attained the age of eight.

There seems to have been a divine purpose in all these sad bereavements. Thrown upon his own resources, Hazrat Muhammad learnt, early in life, the important lessons of self-reliance and social service. The helplessness of orphans and widows made such a deep impression upon the mind of the doubly orphaned child that he showed, throughout life, great sympathy and solicitude for them. This found, when Islam was promulgated, a prominent place in its Scripture, which laid down the care of the orphan and the widow and the service of the poor and the distressed as the essence of religion, and ordained the levy of an income-tax for this purpose.

Earnest and thoughtful, free from boyish levities and frivolities of the age, sweet and gentle in disposition, sober in habits and pleasing in manners and truthful to a fault, this pure-hearted child of the desert commanded the deep attachment and great respect of all who had occasion to come in contact with him. In fact he gave early indication of those noble qualities of head and heart, which raised him high in the estimation of his fellow-beings, among whom he came to be known as "Al-Amin," the Trusty. Book knowledge and school learning he had none. Life in the desert, with its experiences, was all his education. But his natural intelligence, strong commonsense, extraordinary sagacity, unflinching courage and, above all, profound spiritual insight, marked him out as the most outstanding personality the world has ever produced.

Marriage

A fresh chapter opened in Hazrat Muhammad's life when, at the age of twelve, he accompanied his uncle, Abu Talib, who had taken charge of him after his grand-father's death, on a commercial journey to Syria. During the next twelve years he was engaged in business, in which he showed extraordinary capacity, unimpeachable integrity and praiseworthy devotion to duty. Coming to know of his excellent qualities, a kinswoman of his, named Khadija, entrusted him with her trading business. Charmed with his honesty and uprightness, pure character and pleasing manners, she offered him her hand. Although not remarkable for her external charms, twice widowed and older to him by fifteen years, he appreciated the beauty of her heart, and gladly accepted her. The alliance proved a most happy one; for about twenty-seven years nothing disturbed the harmony of their married life.

Arab Society before Islam

The Arabs, at the time we are speaking of, were sunk so low in idolatry, immorality and superstition that no language can give an adequate description of their social disorganisation and spiritual degradation. They had no belief in the life to come and no idea of reward for good and punishment for evil. The sword was unsheathed on the slightest provocation, and blood was shed on the flimsiest pretext. Politically, they were a prey to the inroads of three great powers of the time—the Greeks, the Persians and the Abyssinians—who had subjugated parts of the peninsula and were casting greedy eyes on the rest.

Such was the environment in which Hazrat Muhammad was born. But it did not influence in the least his pure nature. Even as a child he felt great repulsion for every thing obscene, and scrupulously avoided the society of every body whom he thought to be wicked. With the development of his intellectual and moral instincts, the polytheistic rites and superstitious customs of the Quraish, the unbounded lawlessness of the Meccans, the frequent outbursts of sanguinary quarrels among the tribes, the abject politicial subjugation of his motherland—all these roused in his sensitive mind feelings of intense disgust and horror.

Inception of Islam

Freed from the worldly anxieties by his matrimonial alliance, Hazrat Muhammad devoted all his thoughts to social, spiritual and political regeneration of his countrymen. How to purge them of their evil ways and to bring them to the path of piety and righteousness, and how to make them a great nation by uniting the warring tribes and repelling the foreign intruders, became the dream of his life. Agitated by these thoughts, he often retired for prayer and meditation to a cave in the Mount Hira (now called the Mount of Light) near Mecca. There "the great mystery of existence glared in upon him, with its terrors, with its splendours" and there he often stayed days and nights deep in communion with the all-pervading God of the universe.

At last inspiration came from the Lord, the Light, for which he was longing so long, dawned upon him, the inner voice spake unto him. He unmistakably realised that God is great (Allah-o-Akbar), that there is nothing else great, that He is the Reality; all things are but the shadow of Him; that He is the only object of worship; that our whole strength lies in resigned submission to Him; that the service of His creatures is the best means of His adoration. "If you love your Creator, love your fellow-beings first; he is the most favoured of God from whom the greatest good cometh to His creatures.

The more he meditated about religious reform the more was he convinced that the only true religion is pure monotheism, the essence of which is the glorification of God and love of man. It is a fiercely monotheistic religion which admits of no compromise with polytheism. The God of Islam cannot tolerate any sharer in the heart of His adorers.

Islam's Scripture, the Quran, knows no religion that associates anything with God or that is bereft of human sympathy. Islam is in fact another name for the love of the creatures of God for the sake of the love of God*.

Prophet's Persecution

Greatly alarmed and terribly perturbed by an undreamt of onslaught on their cherished faith by one of their own kith and kin, the whole Arab people rose to a man against Hazrat Muhammad. To court martyrdom for one's conviction by bringing death upon oneself in the attempt to establish truth, undoubtedly requires great courage and self-sacrifice. But to keep on living undauntedly amidst immense dangers and disasters and indescribable torments and tortures, worse than death, requires far greater bravery and self-abnegation. For thirteen long years, Hazrat Muhammad persistently held on his path of reform and reproof, preaching Islam with unswerving purpose amidst unremitting persecution of himself and his followers, inhumanly ostracised and boycotted, cruelly tortured and outraged. He,

* It is on account of this uncompromising attitude of Islam in this respect that the Muslim invaders of India could not be absorbed into the Hindu society, as their predecessors, the Greek, the Scythian, the Mongolian and the Parthian invaders, who were partially or completely Hinduised, could be absorbed.

however, all along scrupulously avoided all kinds of retaliation by his followers against the die-hard champions of idolatry and superstition, thus practically demonstrating the principle of non-violence and the path of least resistance, that have been invariably followed in the propagation of Islam. His miraculous escape from his inveterate enemies, determined to put an end to his life in a most fiendish manner and his inevitable migration with a few followers to Yathrib, afterwards named Medina, which was destined to be the centre of Islam's propagation and the place of its prophet's eternal rest, are events of history too well-known to need detailed narration.

In the way to Medina, the Prophet had once to take shelter in a cave where he had Abu Bakr as his only companion. When a number of the enemies passed by that cave, Abu Bakr lost heart and said "the enemies are many while we are only two." "No" the Prophet promptly replied "there is a third, God is with us". Thus on many a critical occasion the Prophet gave indication of his unshakable faith in God.

Battle of Badr

The implacable Quraish idolaters of Mecca would not allow the Muslims peace even in a remote colony. Determined to crush them, they decided to attack them in the place of their shelter. When thus threatened with inevitable annihilation, further persistence in non-resistance would have been nothing short of committing suicide. So the only course left was defensive resistance. Till that time no Muslim had ever drawn his sword in defending his person or property however much he was persecuted. At this juncture a divine revelation was vouchsafed to the Muslims permitting them to take up arms in defence of their lives and their religion.

The inhabitants of Medina, at this time, consisted of the Muhajirin (the exiles), the Ansar (the helpers), the Munafiqin (the disaffected lukewarm converts who retained an ill-concealed predilection for idolatry) and the Jews. The fidelity of the Munafiqin was very doubtful and the Jews, in spite of a pact to join the Muslims in defending Medina against all enemies, secretly helped the Meccans in destroying their fruit trees and carrying away their flocks. Thus were the Muslims compelled, from sheer necessity of the situation and much against their pacific inclination, to take up arms in order to defend themselves. After some foraging raids, a force of one thousand well-equipped Meccans marched towards Medina. Receiving timely information, a body of three hundred believers proceeded to forestall the heathens by occupying the valley of Badr, upon which they were moving. It was only thirty miles from Medina. When Muhammad saw the infidel army arrogantly advancing into the valley, he prayed raising his hands towards heaven, "O Lord forget not Thy promise of assistance. O Lord if this little band were to perish, there will be none to offer unto Thee pure worship". After a fierce fight, the idolaters were driven back with heavy loss, many of their chiefs having fallen in the field of battle.

One of those who took a very active part in the battle of Badr was Abdullah, who came to be called Abu Bakr in history, the constant companion of the Prophet and the first Khalifa after him. His son, who had not embraced Islam, fought against him. When after the battle the son met the father, he told him: "many a time you were within the range of my sword, but I spared you". "I would not have spared you" rejoined the father "had you come within my stroke". This is a typical instance of the fervour and firmness with which the believers braved all sufferings and waived all personal feelings for the sake of their faith.

The victory of Badr gave the Muslims an occasion for displaying the clemency that characterised them. They treated those of their enemies who fell into their hands with such unexampled kindness and courtesy as had never been shown by the victors to their fallen foes in any country or by any nation. Thus was a noble example as regards the treatment of prisoners of war set before the world.

Battle of Uhud

The Quraish could not forget the disgrace of their defeat at Badr. Within a short time they planned another furious attack on the Muslims. After completing the necessary preparations, the resourceful Abu Sufyan, the commander of the Quraish, set out at the head of a well-equipped army of over four thousand to avenge the disaster of Badr. A large body of women accompanied the Quraish army to rouse the spirit of the warriors. Consternation spread among the Muslims when they heard of this unanticipated march of the Quraish. By the time they could decide how to meet the onslaught of their relentless enemies, the Quraish army approached unopposed within a few miles of Medina. Fearing that the siege of the city might place its residents at a great disadvantage, the Prophet sallied out with whatever forces he could hurriedly collect and met the enemies at Uhud, which was only an hour's walk from Medina.

Though outnumbered one to four, the Muslims dauntlessly fell upon the Quraish shouting Allah-ho Akbar. A terrible battle raged for some time, the Muslims fighting furiously with a great heroism born of desperation. Unable to withstand the fury of the Muslims, the idolaters gave way and began to retreat. Seeing this a number of Muslim archers who had been posted at a strategical point to guard the rear, left their post without orders from the Prophet, who himself led the Muslims in this battle, lest they might be too late for the spoils. This gave Khaled, a vigilant Quraish warrior, an excellent opportunity to turn the tide of the battle by a vigorous attack on the Muslim rear. In the confusion that followed, the Prophet got seriously wounded and Hamza, one of his most valiant soldiers, known as "the lion", was slain. Then a rumour that the Prophet was killed proved most destructive to the morale of the Muslims, who began a precipitous retreat. Before long, however, it was found out that the Prophet was alive. This put heart into the Muslims and they succeeded in carving a way to a rocky promotory near by, wherefrom they could defy the enemies. The news of the Prophet's survival so much disheartened the Quraish that although masters of the field at the time, they decided to retire, unable to dislodge the Muslims from their impregnable position. Thus were the Muslims once more saved from imminent annihilation through the grace of Almighty God on whom they entirely relied.

The Quraish committed unheard of barbarities in mutilating the corpses of the Muslims who had fallen in the battle. Abu Sufyan's wife, the ferocious Hinda, is said to have eaten the liver of Hamza and to have worn a necklace made of his entrails, while her inhuman companions cut off the noses and ears of the fallen foes and strung them into garlands. This created a feeling of intense indignation and exasperation among the Muslims and they urged the Prophet to treat the dead enemies in like manner. But the gentleness of his nature conquered the bitterness of their hearts. "Bear wrong patiently", said the Prophet, "verily best will it be for the patiently enduring". From that day the horrible practice of mutilation which prevailed among all people of antiquity, was inexorably forbidden to the Muslims, who treated the Quraish prisoners with kindness and buried with due respect the corpses of the enemies with those of the Muslims.

Two incidents connected with the battle of Uhud, the fiercest battle the Muslims fought during the Prophet's life time, demonstrate the unparallelled affection which his followers entertained for the Prophet. Abu Dujana, one of the generals who led the Muslims at Uhud, displayed unexampled heroism and devotion. When the Prophet was wounded and was in imminent danger of being killed, Abu Dujana shielded him with out-stretched arms, thus making his back a target for the enemies. Pulling out with his own hands the arrows from his back, he handed them over to his comrades to be discharged.

A woman, whose father, husband and son were taking part in the battle of Uhud, went to find out how the battle was proceeding. She enquired of the first man she met on the way what had happened to the Prophet. "Your father has been killed", said the man. "What about the Prophet?" she queried. Your husband has also been killed," was the reply. "What about the Prophet I say?" she rejoined. "Your son too has been slain," said he. "But do tell me, what has happened to the Prophet?" she eagerly demanded. This time the man informed her that the Prophet was safe. Heaving a sigh of relief she exclaimed: "All calamities after thee. O Prophet, are but light". If non-Muslims could have realized the depth of the affection the Muslims bear for their Holy Prophet, they would have understood why some of them go to such extremes in dealing with those who vilify him.

Conquest of Mecca

The indecisive result of the battle of Uhud changed the attitude of the neighbouring Jewish and idolatrous tribes, who would commit outrages on the Muslims whenever they got an opportunity. Thus the Muslims were engaged in skirmishes with non-Muslim tribes throughout the fourth and fifth years of the Hijra. Ultimately the Prophet succeeded in bringing them under control due to the steadfast loyalty of his followers and his own persevering and courageous faith in his divine mission.

In the meantime the Quraish made large preparations for a third invasion of Medina. The Muslims, though worsted in the battle of Uhud, were unbroken in spirit. To a message from Abu Sufyan, the Meccan Chief, that he would come to exterminate the believers, the Prophet's reply was full of trust and faith "Allah is enough for us, a good guardian is he". Sometime after Abu Sufyan marched at the head of a well-equipped army of ten thousand, the largest army that the non-Muslims had ever put in the field. The Jews and other hostile tribes in the adjacent countries readily joined them. While the fate of the Muslims thus hung in the balance, Providence came to their rescue. When the Quraish army was not far from Medina, heavy rains flooded their camp and a terrific hurricane blew away their tents, causing intense panic and havoc in the army and its organisation.

This disastrous calamity so greatly disheartened the Quraish that Abu Sufyan thought it prudent to precepitately return to Mecca. Within a short time, however, the recalcitrant tribes were brought under subjugation and the supremacy of the Muslims was thoroughly established in the country. Henceforth Muslim dominion and sovereignty gradually spread in all directions.

It was now about six years since the Prophet and his faithful followers had left their native land. They longed for a visit to the sacred Kaba at Mecca. The following revelation added to their eagerness :— "you will enter into the Temple of Mecca, if Allah pleases, in security and without fear. Allah knows what you do not know,—He prepares for you a great victory". Concluding a truce with the Quraish, known as the Treaty of Hudaibiya, the Muslims led by the Prophet, peacefully performed the Haj by visiting Mecca and returned unmolested to Medina. The inhabitants of Mecca had, however, been much impressed by the manliness, courtesy,

THE KAABA AT MECCA

kind behaviour and peaceful nature of the Muslims.

Up to this time the message of Islam had been confined to the people of Arabia. Finding his position well-established in his own country, the Prophet thought that the time had come to deliver to other nations the noble message of the religion that was not meant only for the Arabs but was intended to serve as a light and guide to the world at large. Ambassadors were accordingly sent to the courts of Persia, Greece, Egypt, Abyssinia and several other countries. They were honourably received by the rulers of most of these countries, some of whom went so far as to embrace Islam.

Converts now began to pour in from many un-expected quarters. The most important of the new conversions was that of Khalid-ibn-Walid, the non-Muslim victor of Uhud, who soon won fresh laurels by prodigious feats of valour under the banner of Islam. In the conquest of Busra, which took place shortly after his conversion, nine swords are said to have broken in his hands while encountering the Graceo-Roman legions. Henceforth he came to be known as Saifullah, the "Sword of God".

The news of the successes of the Muslims, demonstrating their invincibility, created great consternation in Mecca. Convinced of the futility of further attempts to crush them, the Quraish decided to open negotiations with them and deputed Abu Sufyan to Medina for this purpose. Unsuccessful in getting the desired terms, Abu Sufyan hastened back to Mecca to advise his people to make peaceful submission to the all-conquering Prophet.

Shortly after, the Muslims under their Prophet marched upon Mecca and arrived unopposed at its gate. There some of the Quraish battalions disputed the passage of the Muslims but had soon to give way. Thus on Friday the 21st day of the month of Ramadan in the ninth year of the Hijra, corresponding to 631st of the Christian era, seven years after his migration, Hazrat Muhammad made his victorious entry into Mecca with ten thousand of his followers. The first thing he did was to break the three hundred gods who had usurped Allah's place in Kaaba and to purge the shrine of all profanities. He then addressed the vast multitude in the verses of the Quran: "There is only one God. He has fulfilled his promises and brought success to His worshippers. He also has confounded the enemy and defeated its battalions. He gave me authority over you in order to make you abjure idolatry. You shall no longer accord honour to insensible stones. You shall no longer practise sacrilegious cults".

The relentless persecutors of the Prophet, who had sworn to take his life, and subjected him to untold barbarities, indignities and even physical privations and tortures and had driven him away from home, now lay prostrate at his feet. No punishment would have been too severe for such fiendish foes. In those days a conquest by the might of arms carried with it the right to reduce the conquered to bondage, to forfeit their property and to put to death the leading captives. Besides, there were no extenuating circumstances justifying indulgence on this occasion to the inhuman Quraish. But the merciful Prophet refrained from taking any of the customary penal steps of war. "What have you to say as to how I should treat you?" he asked the Quraish. "As the generous brother that you are," they replied. "So be it" he said, "I will not reproach you to-day. You are free, for God has forgiven you". The general amnesty included even Abu Sufyan, who was at the root of the indescribable sufferings of the Muslims, and his wife, Hinda, who had chewed the liver of Hamza. This unparallelled clemency in the hour of triumph shown by Hazrat Muhammad to the relentless Quraish is an event unique in human history, setting as it did, a noble example to the world as to how to treat one's fallen enemies and to forgive and love humanity even at its worst.

The unexampled self-restraint and scrupulous regard for their pledged word displayed by the Muslims made such a deep impression upon the idolaters that hosts upon hosts flocked to the Prophet and embraced Islam, giving a solemn pledge that "they would not worship gods of polytheists, but one only God, they would not commit larceny, adultery and infanticide, they would not utter falsehood, nor speak ill of women."

Islam thus accomplished what had never before been achieved either by Judaism or Christianity, both of which had long tried to wean the Arab tribes from their gross superstition, their inhuman practices and their licentious immorality. Idolatry was completely shattered and the all-pervading moral and spiritual darkness in which Arabia was enshrouded from time immemorial was at last lifted for ever. The people were purged of the superstition, cruelty and vice in which they were steeped. Under the Prophet's banner the scattered tribes of Arabia became a united nation. Filled with great ardour and enthusiasm, which imparted an almost invincible strength to their arms, they poured forth over three continents to conquer and subdue in the name of the Lord.

Death of the Prophet.

In the sixty-third year of his life and tenth year of the Hijra, Hazrat Muhammad's health began to decline. At this time the death of his only surviving son, the little Ibrahim, gave him a very great shock. This smashed whatever interest he had left in worldly life. When he found his end was drawing nigh, he thought of making a last pilgrimage to the sacred Kaaba,. He started for Mecca early in 632 A.D. Coming to know of this, a vast concourse of pilgrims, said to be a lak and a quarter, the largest Mecca had ever seen, congregated there. On the completion of the pilgrimage, the Prophet delivered to the assembled pilgrims a sublime message, which concluded thus :—"Fix this in your hearts that every Muslim is the brother of every other Muslim. You are all equal, enjoying equal rights and subject to the same obligations. It is accordingly forbidden to you to take from your brother save that which he gives you of his own free will".

On his return to Medina the Prophet fell ill. After suffering for some days from fever he breathed his last on the 7th June 632 A.D., and plunged the whole of Muslim Arabia into profound grief. He did not nominate any successor to the apostolic headship of Islam, but left the selection to the choice of the Muslims of Medina. Hazrat Abu Bakr was thereupon acclaimed as the head of the Muslims. On his death Hazrat Omar was elected his successor, and when he was assassinated, Hazrat Osman took his place. He fell a victim to party faction and was killed. Hazrat Ali, the Prophet's cousin and the husband of his favourite daughter, Fatima,* was the last of the four illustrious apostolic heads who are known as Khulafai Rashidin. The Shia sect of the Muslims denounce the first three Khalifas, holding that by lineage and capacity Hazrat Ali was entitled to succeed as the first Khalifa.

The mission of Hazrat Muhammad was thoroughly accomplished. He not only expounded theories like the Prophets who had gone before him, but had opportunities of testing their efficacy in practice. Of all the great teachers of the world, he was the only one who achieved in his life time the whole of the work he had envisaged. He alone had the satisfaction of seeing the fruition of his efforts for the spiritual, moral and material uplift of his people and of humanity at large. In this fact lies his superiority over the prophets and philosophers

* By his first wife, Khadija, the Prophet had two sons, Qasim the first born, after whom Khadija used to call her husband Abul Qasim, and another son, the last born, who did not live, and four daughters—Zainab, Ruqayya, Ummi-Kultum and Fatima. Qasim died in his infancy. Fatima was the most beloved child.

of other times and other nations. Gautama, Zoroaster, Moses, Jesus, Plato, Socrates all had to leave the world almost as they found it; they departed with their aspirations unfulfilled, their bright visions unrealized. They had to bequeathe the task of spreading their religions and thereby elevating their fellow men to their powerful disciples —a Joshua among the Israelites, an Asoka among the Buddhists, a Constantine among the Christians. It was reserved for Hazrat Muhammad alone to fulfil his mission himself, to see the work of moral, social, and even political amelioration very largely accomplished. No royal disciple came to his assistance with edicts to enforce his teaching; the entire work may be said to have been the work of God. Within the space of nine years he lifted up his people from the depth of moral and spiritual degradation to a high conception of God, of morality, of purity, of justice; and he ineffaceably impressed the unity of God, and the equality of man upon the minds of all the peoples with whom he had occasion to come in contact.

After the Prophet's death, particularly during the Khilafat of Hazrat Omar, Islam spread with amazing rapidity, overwhelming some of the long-established religions of the world and shattering some of the mightiest monarchies of the time, such as those of Palestine, Egypt, North Africa, Persia. The other great religions won their way slowly, by hard struggles and some with the aid of powerful monarchs. But Islam springing from a desert land, among an unadventurous people, unknown to history, miraculously triumphed against heavy odds, with slender human backing and in less than a century extended its sway from the Guadelquiver in the west to the Indus in the east. "A poor shepherd people" says Carlyle "roaming unnoticed in its deserts since the creation of the world; a Hero-Prophet was sent down to them with a word they could believe: see the unnoticed becomes world-notable, the small has grown world-great, within one century afterwards, Arabia is at Granada on this hand, at Delhi on that; glancing in valour and splendour and the light of genius, Arabia shines through long ages over a great section of the world".

Character.

Of all the Prophets of old, Hazrat Muhammad is the only historical personage every detail of whose life, from the cradle to the grave, is thoroughly known to the whole world. There was no other prophet whose life history is so well-known and of whose actions and sayings such detailed authentic records exist. His chequered career, in contradistinction to that of other prophets before him, embraced almost all the phases of human life. He was a beloved orphan, a devoted husband, an affectionate father, a successful business man, a far-sighted reformer, an impressive preacher, a patient fugitive, a brave warrior, a skilful general, a merciful conqueror, an efficient administrator, an impartial judge, an ideal law-giver, a great statesman, and a ruler of extraordinary capacity. In all these roles he played his part with such exemplary ability, honesty, integrity, courage, foresight, patience, perseverance and devotion to duty as to be marked out as an outstanding ideal to mankind. It can be truly said of him that he "left nothing untouched and touched nothing which he did not rectify and improve". In fact in his noble person were combined all the virtues and excellences of all other prophets. He was ever ready to help the orphan, to relieve the needy, and to ransom the slave. He never sought revenge; he always took delight in forgiving and in showing mercy even to his bitterest enemies. In these respects perhaps the world has never seen his like. Within the short space of ten years he brought about changes which have given an entirely new direction to the history of mankind.

There is nothing mysterious, nothing supernatural about Hazrat Muhammad. He was a mere man, "I am naught but a man like unto you," he declared to the lowest of the low. In mundane matters he never claimed to be infallible, to be above human limitations. Lest his followers, like the followers of other religions, should feel inclined to deify him, he added to, "La Ilaha Illallah," (there is no god, but God), "Muhammadur Rasul-Allah" (Muhammad is a Messenger of God) as an ever recurring reminder; though some of his ungenerous critics regard even this as associating himself with God. He is repeatedly addressed in the Quran as, "Abduhu wa Rasuluh". He was a mere messenger, a servant of the Lord, commissioned to carry out His instructions for the reclamation, for the reformation, for the elevation of His creatures. And how well and faithfully did he serve humanity in pursuance of his Lord's command. To liberate man, to unite man, to educate man, to elevate man, in a word, to humanise man was the sole mission of his life. Never in the vicissitudes of his chequered career did this all-dominating passion for the service of humanity abate even for a moment. The regal sceptre which usually intoxicates man, failed to work any change in the man in Muhammad. The uncrowned king of Arabia, that he undoubtedly was, he would stitch his own clothes, mend his own shoes, tend his own cattle, milk his own goats, and even sweep the floor of his house. When a mosque was being constructed at Medina, he carried the bricks on his head. Once some one seeing him bleeding having been pelted by some of his inhuman tormentors, suggested imprecation, but the man in Muhammad revolted against the idea of imprecation even when he was in such a predicament. "I am not sent as a curse to mankind," said he, "I am sent as a blessing unto humanity". On another occasion when a Jew was very rude to him in demanding repayment of money which he had lent him, Omar, who was present there, got very much enraged. "That is not fair Omar," protested the Prophet, "You ought to have advised me to pay the money and the Jew to be more gentle in his demands". While he was on his deathbed he had it announced, "If there is any one whom I have wronged, let him come forward and avenge the wrong while I am yet alive".

The history of the human race cannot present another man who was a model for his fellow creatures in every sphere of life. The unique personality of Hazrat Muhammad, the torch bearer of divine truth for all countries and all peoples, presents a most enchanting picture, look at it from whatever angle we would. From an orphan boy and then a persecuted refugee to a powerful overlord, spiritual as well as temporal, of a whole nation, is a panorama of exquisite beauty that fails not to fascinate the onlooker even through this distance of time. Whatever part he was called upon by circumstances to play, he invariably played it like a great hero, shedding unearthly lustre on the whole game. Whatever position he was called upon to fill, he made it so brilliantly glorious, that the history of man has no parallel to present. As an apostle, as a reformer, as a general, as a conqueror, as a king, as a legislator—in all these illustrious roles the halo of the hero shines brightly on his face. But in this whole picture there is nothing like Muhammad the man. It is the man in Muhammad that marks the prettiest spot in this all-round exquisitely beautiful portrait. It is the human touch in all that he was and in all that he did that lends the whole scene an unsurpassable grace.

Such was Hazrat Muhammad, whose humanity was the most invincible force of his personality and the strongest testimony to the truth of his mission. Bosworth Smith truly observed, "Muhammad to the end of his life claimed for himself that title only with which he had begun, and the highest philosophy and the truest Christianity will one day, I venture to believe, agree in yielding to him that of a Prophet, a very Prophet of God". Carlyle was well-justified when addressing the western world, he exclaimed "To call such a man an impostor is an insult to their intelligence". Lamartine, the well-known French poet and prose writer, was perfectly right when after referring to Hazrat Muhammad as a "philosopher, orator, apostle, warrior, legislator, conqueror of ideas, restorer of dogmas, founder of empires," queried, "By all the standards with which one measures human greatness, what man was greater?" "None," I have no doubt, will be the answer of the world to this pertinent query. History cannot cite a greater personality judged by any standard of human greatness.

The followers of the Prophet, whose religion does not lay undue stress on any abstract ethical code, look upon him as a perfect exemplar, a concrete ethical code, as it were, for their guidance. To a Muslim whatever his Prophet thought was right, whatever he said was right, whatever he did was right, and Muslims have simply to follow him in thought, word and deed. Muslims believe that their Holy Prophet was imbued with divine attributes and he lived in perfect harmony with them.

———

*

CHAPTER II

HAZRAT MUHAMMAD AS A RELIGIOUS REFORMER

Religion is the recognition of a Supreme Being with supernatural powers, and the performance of man's duties of love and obedience towards Him. Since his very creation Man had to realise the existence of such a Being as the Creator of the universe.

Man is perhaps the greatest and the grandest handi-work of the Supreme Being, generally known as God. But he is a complex creature, an amalgam of brutishness and divinity, half animal and half divine. There are in him germs of all that is good and great as well as of all that is evil and ignoble. By developing the former potentialities he can raise himself to the highest of the high and by developing the latter he may degrade himself to the lowest of the low. While by the exercise of his moral and spiritual qualities he can surpass even the angels and approach the borders of Divinity, by indulging in his carnal passions he may drag himself down to a level lower than that of brutes. Thus man has capacity for unlimited moral and spiritual progress as well as for unbounded iniquity and animalism. Firm faith in God may elevate man to a state of heavenly bliss and prevent him from being led to the abyss of iniquity and impurity.

Prophets.—To initiate man into these mysteries and to teach him how to develop and exercise his capacity for moral and spiritual progress and how to check and control his evil passions and propensities, God was pleased to send, from time to time, inspired teachers known as Prophets. Thus there appeared among all nations in different ages and in different climes, Messengers of God for the instruction and uplift of mankind.

Tribal Prophets.—For want of inter-communication among different isolated people due to geographical barriers, the earlier Messengers were intended for particular nations and particular countries, and their teachings were exclusively adapted to the peculiar needs and conditions of these tribes. What they—Noah, Abraham, Moses, David, Solomon, Jesus—had taught was in course of time corrupted, and unwarranted interpolations found place in the Scriptures revealed through them. That some of these Scriptures had to be "modernised" from time to time in order to make their teachings suitable to changed circumstances, unmistakably shows that they were not intended for all time.

Universal Prophet.—Change of world circumstances enabling people of distant countries to meet and exchange thoughts and ideas made the appearance of a universal Messenger at a central place, with a message for the whole of mankind, essentially necessary. A religion of peace and progress that would have brought peace to the world by uniting the warring tribes under a common faith and would have ushered in an era of cultural progress by furthering the cause of science and civilisation, was the crying need of the time. The advent of such a Messenger for the propagation of a universal religion was not unanticipated. It had been foreshadowed by some of the previous Messengers of God. "The piety of Moses and of Christ" truly says John Davenport "rejoiced in the assurance of a future prophet more illustrious than themselves, and the Evangelists' promise of a paraclete, or Holy Ghost, the Comforter, was prefigured in the name and accomplished in the person of the greatest and last of God's prophets." To Asia, the cradle of prophets and patriarchs, of saints and sages, belongs the credit of producing this great Messenger whose noble message of the unity of God and equality of man served, more than anything else did before or after, to bring about the uplift of the human race and to establish peace and good will on earth.

The Prophet of Arabia, Hazrat Muhammad, also called Ahmad, was the "greatest and last of God's Prophets" referred to by Davenport. His predecessor was Jesus Christ, after whom no Prophet worth mentioning, appeared for about six hundred years. During this period unthought of demoralisation took place in the world. Hazrat Muhammad's advent, therefore, synchronised with a time when intellectual sterility and spiritual stagnation prevailed all over the world. Arabia was perhaps in a worse condition than any other country. Drunkenness, debauchery, gambling, rapacity, blood-thirstiness and such other heinous vices were rampant among the Arabs. In fact there was hardly any vice to which they were not passionately addicted. These were the people of all peoples who most required for their regeneration personal instruction by an inspired teacher.

The prevailing religions had greatly deteriorated, unthought of corruptions having crept into them in course of time. Originally one supreme immaterial God was the object of adoration in most of these religions, but in course of time material representation in some form or other came to be worshipped as god. Besides, the various sects into which these religions got subdivided in course of time began to fight one another very bitterly. Thus religion ceased to be a fountain-head of peace and order, as was originally intended, and came to be a mere pretext for disorder, anarchy and even war.

Pondering over this deplorable condition of the people of the world, Hazrat Muhammad came to the conclusion that such a religion was required for their reclamation as would elevate and not demoralise humanity, would reconstruct and not destroy society, would unite and not divide people. The more Hazrat Muhammad meditated about religious reform the more was he convinced that pure monotheism, the essence of which is the glorification of God and love of man, is the true religion. He decided to promulgate such a religion.

What is Islam

Islam is not, as is generally believed by non-Muslims, the religion of Hazrat Muhammad in the sense in which Buddhism is the religion of Buddha and Christianity is the religion of Christ. "Muhammadanism" is in fact a misnomer. It has no place in the nomenclature of Islamic history. The word is a creation of the medieval literature of Europe, coined on the analogy of Christianity. "Muhammadanism," if it means anything, may mean that phase of Islam which was promulgated and preached by Prophet Muhammad.

Islam, which is entire submission of man to absolute sovereignty of God and peace with Him and His creatures, was the religion of all true Prophets, the religion of Adam, of Abraham, of Moses, of Jesus. Every true religion, by whatever name it might have been called, originally came from God and every true Prophet was deputed by Him to teach the same eternal truth.

Din and Madhhab

Religion consists of two parts, viz., *Din* (religion) and *Madhhab* (pathway), the abstract and the concrete. While *Din* represents the fundamental conception or creed of man about the universe and its Creator, *Madhhab* denotes the complex of rules, customs, conventions and institutions which govern human life in its manifold spheres. While *Din* in its nature has always been one and universal, absolute and permanent, *Madhhab* has largely been divergent, local, temporary and conditional in its character. Thus every Prophet while proclaiming the same Din, had to adopt a different *Madhhab* in order to meet the particular requirements of time, place, stage of human development and specific requirements of different peoples, separated from one another by the barriers of geographical, racial, national, cultural, linguistic and political divisions.

With the advent of the Prophet of Arabia the period of national prophets and local *Madhhabs* came to an end. He removed all misinterpretations and corruptions that had crept into different *Madhhabs* and evolved a perfected and universalised *Madhhab*. Islam may, therefore, be said to be the fulfilment and completion of all previous religions. Thus in essentials there is hardly any difference between Islam and Christianity shorn of all man-made dogmas. This does not mean that humanity has reached a finality and there is no scope for further moral or religious evolution. It merely means that *Madhhab* has now passed from the limited, local and national stage to the universal and permanent stage requiring only minor modifications in non-essentials to suit all ages and all climes.

Formation of different religious sects.

Many people for want of proper education and correct information, failed to realise the true import and implication of *Din* and of *Madhhab*. They mistook the forms and formulae, rites and rituals of *Madhhab* for real *Din*. Thus thy differed in their religious belief and formed different religious sects, each one of which proclaimed that they were the chosen people of the Lord and they alone were entitled to salvation. So, there arose bitter religious controversies and quarrels which brought dissension and disruption to the human race. Islam put a stop to this by proclaiming that ever since the beginning of human habitation on the surface of the earth there has been only one *Din* revealed by God to His Prophets; it was only their Madhhabs that were different. Salvation, therefore, does not lie in joining a particular religious group or labelling oneself by the name of a particular sect, but in realising and practising the spirit of real *Din* in thoughts, words and deeds.

According to Islam heavenly light was given to all nations; there is no country and no community that did not receive a Messenger from God. Different religions represent different angles from which man looks at the Lord. The goal is invariably the same, though the means of seeking it may be different. Islam is not, therefore, a new religion; it is the old religion that was proclaimed by all the Prophets who appeared before the Prophet of Arabia at different times and in different climes. But for the deterioration and adulteration that took place in their teachings in course of time, there would have been no difference between religion and religion.

All that Islam claims is that it has purged the impurities and adulterations that crept into former religions.

The Scripture of Islam.

The Scripture of Islam, the Quran, is an unsectarian revelation for the whole of mankind. It is not a mere collection of dogmas, like the scriptures of other religions, nor a voluminous treatise on theism, but a code of life. It is a social, civil, judicial, military, penal, commercial and yet a religious code, which regulates everything which a human being has to do for his welfare from the cradle to the grave. The whole of it was not revealed all at once, but was sent down piece-meal during the space of twenty-three years. Whenever an incident occurred requiring divine guidance the angel Gabriel brought down a verse or a few verses to enlighten the Holy Prophet.

Though the Quran gives solution to all important problems of human life, and provides for every contingency of human affairs, it is wonderfully laconic, the whole of its teachings having been condensed into 9,666 verses. It is the master-piece of the Arabic language and is extolled throughout the world for the simple grandeur of its diction, the chaste elegance of its style and the variety and magnificence of its imageris, all of which are altogether inimitable. "The most remarkable feature of the Quran wherein not a hole could be picked", writes Dr. Maurice, who translated the Quran into French "is its perfect diction and wonderful eloquence. The marvellous superiority of the Book of Allah to all others, in which forty crores of people do rightly and justly take pride, is that in point of the most pure and noble objects promulgated by the Book and the exquisite arrangement of sublime ideas, this Book surpasses all other Books revealed from on High". "The Quran presents a perfect and complete code of all tenets and doctrines and principles and morals as well as the laws based thereon," writes Ludolf Krall, "it contains the most comprehensive basis for all the rules and regulations for a vast democracy, for governance and administration, for justice and equity, for military organisation, for financial equipment and stability and for the proper control and guidance of the rich and poor, classes and masses, and the rulers and the ruled alike". "The Quran is undoubtedly by far the most authentic book of the Arabic language," writes George Sale, the well-known translator of the Quran, albeit a bigoted critic, "and such is the belief of the most pious Muslims, and the Book teaches them likewise, that no mortal could possibly pen such a miraculous book. It is indeed a perfect miracle by itself, which is far more sublime than the mere act of resuscitating the dead; and this Book *per se* is enough to convince the sceptic of its being a Revelation from on High . . . . Its verses are most eloquent, particularly those in which the attributes of God are mentioned, even though my translation may not convey to the reader the exquisite beauty of the original". "The Quran enjoys the distinction of having been the starting point of a new literary and philosophical movement which has powerfully affected the finest and the most cultivated minds among both Jews and Christians in the middle ages," Rev. Margolliouth.

Unlike the scriptures of other religions, the Quran has come down to us in its pristine purity, genuine, undefiled and unchallenged. Its inspiration is the only miracle to which the Prophet lays claim. Failing to produce from the whole range of their language and literature, which had already reached a very high level of perfection, anything that could approach a single verse of the Quran, the Arab idolaters had to desist from questioning its divine origin. After thirteen centuries it still remains an unerring guide to humanity. It is the sobriety of the life imposed by the precepts of the Quran that preserved the general mass of Muslims from those wild outbursts which disgraced the lives of the followers of some other religions; the moderation of speech and the respect for law and property formed a safeguard to the world against oppression.

The teaching of the Quran is purely rational; there is nothing dogmatic in it. It inculcates the noblest ideals of monotheism, universalism, democracy, unity and fraternity. It was the first in the field to proclaim the unity of God and the equality of man. It is a refutation of the doctrine of original sin, which makes man devoid of all excellence at birth. It establishes the inherent sinlessness of man's nature, which, according to it, is capable of unlimited progress, setting man above the angels and leading him to the border of divinity.

The Unities of Islam

The three basic unities on which the entire structure of the Quranic message may be said to have been founded are (1) Tauhid-i-Ummat, oneness of the nationality of mankind; (2) Tauhid-i-Rabu-biat, Oneness of the Rab, the Creator, Sustainer, Evolver and Guardian of all; (3) Tauhid-i-ibadat, oneness of worship and the singleness of the Almighty to Whom all should submit and surrender their entire selves. Although the difference of country, colour, race and language have divided mankind into thousands of groups, they all constitute only one family of the house of Adam and Eve and one nationality of the human genus. The one absolute eternal reality of God cannot be changed by giving him different names in different languages and by worshipping him by different methods in different temples. When man's Creator is one, he should recognise His absolute sovereignty and worship Him and surrender himself to Him alone.

Islam, an Ideal Religion

It is a remarkable fact that the three great monotheistic religions of the world—Judaism, Christianity and Islam sprang from the confines of the Arabian Peninsula, the Jaziratul-Arab. The prophetic impulse which the course of history had called from among the people of the Israel gave birth to all of them. Both Judaism and Christianity found acceptance with some of the people of Arabia. Long before the advent of Hazrat Muhammad there were Jews in Arabia, and when Christianity was preached, it was embraced by some of the Arab tribes. But neither the intricately elaborate Judaism nor the highly sophisticated Christianity of Greek speculation and dogmatism could make much headway in the idolatrous peninsula. On the contrary, they were themselves much affected by Arab idolatry. They, however, played their part in preparing the spiritual soil of Arabia for the enthusiastic reception of monotheistic Islam. Their failure to capture the Arabs was a convincing proof that it was not an esoteric religion, with intricate rituals, contentious dogmas, questionable principles and unattainable ideals, that could regenerate a demoralised people, but a simple, rational, practical, and yet ideal religion that could be easily followed in every day life. Such a religion is Islam which is not merely to be loved but to be lived, and is "essentially rationalistic in the widest sense of the term, considered etymologically and historically."

Islam swept away all corruption and superstition. It was, in fact, a revolt against empty theological polemics. It brought out the fundamental dogmas of religion—the unity and greatness of God, that He is merciful and righteous, that He claims obedience to His will, resignation and faith. "Islam proclaimed," writes Canon Taylor, "the responsibility of man, a future life, a day of judgment, and stern retribution to fall upon the wicked, and enforced the duties of prayer, almsgiving, fasting and benevolence. It thrust aside the artificial virtues, the religious frauds and follies, the perverted moral sentiments and the verbal subtleties of theological disputants. It gave hope to the slave, brotherhood to mankind and recognition to the fundamental facts of human nature".

Simplicity of Islam

One of the distinctive features of Islam is its simplicity. Its teaching is not shrouded in myths and stories and has nothing mysterious, nothing irrational, nothing impractical, nothing unattainable in it. It strongly appeals to the intellect as well as to the natural sentiments engrafted in human nature. It is in perfect harmony with science and may be said to have been writ large on the face of Nature from the gigantic sun to the tiniest blade of grass. According to Islam every atom in the universe, while maintaining the general equilibrium, is incessantly busy proclaiming that submission to the Will of Almighty God is the only religion throughout the universe. What scientists call Laws of Nature is, in religious phraseology, the Will of the Lord, which may be read in His Book of Nature. Islam is nothing but complete submission to God's Will. "Is it then other than God's religion that they seek (to follow) and to Him submits whatever is in the heavens and the earth willingly or unwillingly and to Him shall they be returned." Al-Quran.

"Foremost among the causes that contributed to the success of Islam" writes Arnold "was the simplicity of the Muslim creed. There is no God but God; Muhammad is the apostle of God. Assent to these two simple doctrines is all that is demanded of the convert. This simple creed demands no great trial of faith and is within the compass of the meanest intelligence. Unencumbered with theological subtleties, it may be expounded by any, even the most unversed in theological expression. The first half of it enunciates a doctrine that is almost universally accepted by men as a necessary postulate, while the second half is based on a theory of man's relationship to God that is almost equally wide-spread, viz. that at intervals in the world's history God grants some revelation of Himself to men through the mouthpiece of inspired Prophets". "A creed so precise, so stripped of all theological complexities and consequently so accessible to the ordinary understanding," observes Professor Montel, "might be expected to possess, and does indeed possess, a marvellous power of winning its way into the consciences of men". "The creed of Muhammad is free from suspicion or ambiguity, and the Quran is a glorious testimony of the unity of God . . . . A philosophic theist might subscribe to the popular creed of the Muhammadans: a creed too sublime perhaps for our present faculties," says Gibbon.

This is Islam, a religion so simple, so natural, so practical and, at the same time, so sublime. It is but natural that such an ideal religion should inspire its followers with a fervour and firmness unparalleled in the annals of religion. The cultivators quitting their ploughs and prostrating themselves in the field, the labourers throwing down their burdens and squatting on the street, when the time for prayer comes, are unique sights, unknown and unseen in any country other than those with a Muslim population. Besides, history has no instance to cite approaching the glorious ideals of catholicity, toleration, equality and fraternity which Islam has set before the world. It is these unique features of Islam that enabled it so suddenly to emerge out of the chaos of centuries and to establish itself in an incredibly short span of only about three decades as a strong power which shook the mighty empires of the Caesars and the Khosroes. Is not the wonderful progress that Islam later on made in different countries of the globe, among various peoples, numbering about one-third of the whole human race, an unmistakable proof of its inherent vitality, its excellence, its catholicity, its adaptibility, its universality?

Universality of Islam

Islam laid the foundation of universalism in religion. This is its most distinctive feature. It is as wide in its conception as humanity. It is not meant for one people or for one country or for one age. The very first verse of the Quran proclaims the oneness of all people. There God has been described as "Rabbul Alamin," the Creator, the Nourisher and the Guide of all, not as the God of Israel or any other particular nation. Nowhere has it been stated that God is "Rabbul-Muslimin," the Lord of the Muslims only. "Surely those who believe and those who are Jews and the Christians, and the Sabians, whoever believes in God and the Last Day and does good, they shall have their reward from their Lord and there is no fear for them, nor shall they grieve." "And they say none shall enter Paradise except he who is a Jew or Christian. These are their fancies. Say bring your proof if you are truthful. Yea, whoever submits himself to God and he is the doer of good (to others), he has reward from his Lord, and there is no fear for him, nor shall be grieve." Al-Quran.

Thus according to Islam the goal of all true religions is invariably the same, though the means of its attainment may be different. In this respect the Quran is in agreement with the Bhagawat Gita in which the Lord says "Mankind comes to Me along many roads and on whatever road a man approaches Me on that road do I welcome him, for all roads are Mine." It is hoped that one day Islam will be the religion of all humanity as it is the only religion that appeals to human reason and possesses the width and elasticity essential for a world religion.

Islam enjoins respect for all Prophets

A Muslim under the categorical injunctions of the Quran, can make no distinction between one medium of light and another. Faith in all the teachers sent by God to man is the fourth of the "Seven Articles of Islamic Faith". So every Muslim has to believe in all the Prophets and the Scriptures that were sent by God from time to time. Side by side with his Holy Prophet, he is required to regard all other messengers of God—Moses, Jesus, and others—as worthy of love and veneration. "We believe in God and that which hath been sent down to us, and that which hath been given to Abraham and Isaac and Jacob, and the tribes, and that which hath been given to Moses and Jesus and that which was given to the Prophets from their Lord. No distinction do we make between any of them, and to God we are resigned". "And certainly we sent apostles before you (Muhammad): there are some of them that we have mentioned to you, and there are others whom we have not mentioned to you". "They who say we believe in some of the apostles and reject others and seek to take a middle course in the matter, they are really unbelievers, and we have prepared for the unbelievers an ignominous punishment. But they who believe in God and His apostles, and make no distinction between any of them, unto these we surely give their reward; and God is gracious and merciful". Al- Quran. The exceuse for this long quotation is the necessity of stressing the sanctity of all the Prophets and impressing it not only upon those who do not know it, but also upon those who, in their fanatical zeal, are apt to overlook it.

Mediation has no place in Islam

Every one, according to Islam is solely responsible for his own actions. While on the one hand, man is not held in any way responsible for what he does not actually do himself, on the other there can be no expiation by another person for what he does. According to Islam man is born sinless; he is not at all accountable for the sins of his ancestors. Nor can he get his own sins expiated by others. Islam thus engenders in every one of its followers a sense of personal responsibility and does not recognise any mediator between man and God. A Muslim is directly accountable to his Lord for all that he thinks or says or does, and he has himself to work out his salvation by his own good deeds without the intervention of mediators. Islam recognises no priest-craft and it knows no intermediary who can grant a Muslim a free passport to heaven. The claim of the Hindu Brahmin, the Buddhist Phungi, the Jewish Rabi and the Christian Padri, to stand between man and God, is regarded by Islam as the height of arrogance. The best among the Muslims automatically becomes the leader in a congregation or conference. Among the Muslims there are no priests, no virgins, no monks, no nuns. There is no need for candles or masses, and no tolls have to be paid on the road to heaven.

Islam, a Religion of Worldly People

Man is a social animal. He requires, for his guidance, a religion that concerns actual worldly affairs more than anything else. Such a religion is Islam, which enjoins man to live in the world and to serve its denizens. It is not intended for the anchorites, who shun the world and lead an isolated retired life.

The whole outlook of Islam regarding life is based on a virile optimism and masculine positivism. Islam regards life as a positive good and great opportunity for evolution to higher and higher planes of existence, not as an evil, as a bondage, a blind and relentless cycle of births and rebirths from which there appears no Mukti (salvation) but self-mortification. Hence renunciation, self-mortification, suicide, virginity, forced widowhood and monasticism are totally forbidden as anti-human and anti-social evils which have no place in a true religion. The practical result of this virile and optimistic conception of life is that man, who is equal to his brother, second only to God and superior to everything else, must conquer the whole universe, the seen and unseen worlds, and enjoy life to the fullest extent for evolution to higher planes bordering on divinity.

Islam has made family life the basis of social organisation, holding martrimony essential for social purity and peace and for the general welfare of mankind. Maintenance of family and rearing of children have been ordained as imperative duties of man. To be a dutiful son, a faithful husband and an affectionate father are to be counted as great virtues. Thus has Islam sanctified every detail of mundane life, and this is one of its most distinctive features.

Islam has put a ban on celibacy and renunciation of the world. While Christian doctors try to combat the licentiousness of the age by setting forth the celestial merit of celibacy and the angelic virtue of virginity, Islam put in a strong protest against the exaltation of celibacy as a ground for fighting licentiousness. It thrust aside artificial virtue and replaced monkishness by manliness. According to it man's glory is not in killing his natural passions, but in controlling them and utilising them for the good of humanity. 'Discipline your powers' is the message of the Quran, while 'kill your natural desires' is the message of other religions. Thus has Islam made a life of service and sacrifice within the world the crown of human existence.

Catholicity of Islam

In its catholicity Islam stands altogether unrivalled. It looks upon all people as members of one family and holds that all religions lead to the same goal. It aims at creating amity and good understanding among the followers of various persuasions. It does not allow its followers to take pride in race, colour or country. The Muslims all the world over are knit together by a common bond of brotherhood. Slaves become kings and kings condescend to stand shoulder to shoulder with beggars in rags.

It is a regrettable fact that race, colour, country and language prejudices are sapping the very life of humanity. Africans are being lynched in America simply because they happen to be black, although the white there profess to be of the same religion. This would not have happened if the Americans had been Muslims.

Islam is not mere prayer, or fasting, or keeping up of so many other rites and rituals; it is playing the game of life as Hazrat Muhammad played it, attending to the duties to God and man, and leading a virtuous life. "It is not righteousness that you turn your faces towards the east and the west; but righteousness is this that one shall believe in God and the Last Day and the angels and the Book and the Prophets, and give away wealth out of love for Him to the near of kin and the orphans and the needy and the way-farer and the beggars and for the emancipation of the captives, and keep up prayer and pay the poor rate, and the performers of their promise when they make a promise and the patient in distress and affliction and in time of conflict—these are they who are true (to themselves) and these are they who are pious." Thus according to the

Quran, a non-Muslim, be he a Jew or a Christian, a Hindu or a Buddhist, who lives a Muhammad-like life of truth, of piety, of honesty, who maintains a family, takes care of the orphan and the widow, helps the poor and the destitute, is a practical follower of the Prophet, whereas one bearing a Muslim name, but leading a vicious life, and acting contrary to Quranic injunctions, is not a true Muslim, rather a walking libel on the good name of Islam and its Holy Prophet. In fact one cannot be a true Muslim unless one is a very good man. There are many true Muslims without knowing it themselves.

To judge Islam by the behaviour of many of its present-day followers would be doing it a great injustice. True Islam, which is life and light, is very different from what goes by its name to-day—a bundle of dead rituals and meaningless ceremonies. True Islam broadens the outlook and provides ample scope for honest differences of opinion. But the generality of the present-day Muslims, leaving aside the essentials of their faith, are engaged in acrimonious controversies over mere trifles—petty questions of details. What can be more regrettable than the fact that Muslims do not hesitate to fly at each other's throats over a word, nay even over the pronunciation of a word, such as *Daallin* and *Zaallin,* and a voice raised or suppressed on particular occasions in prayers leads to actual blood-shed. Besides Sunnis and Shias, there are now in India various sects, such as Hanafis, Kadianis, Ahl-i-Hadis, whose unseemly wranglings reflect much discredit on Islam. They do not join each other in prayers and feel no scruple in calling each other Kafirs.

Islam seems to be passing through a crisis, particularly in Bengal, which has more Muslims than in a similar area anywhere in the world. Two opposite forces have formed, as it were, an unholy alliance against it. On the one hand narrow-minded theologians, generally known as Mullas, who overlook the essentials of their noble religion and attach undue importance to its minor details, feel no hesitation in pronouncing Fatwas of Kufr on the slightest deviation from them, as if their mission is to make Muslims Kafirs and not Kafirs Muslims. On the other hand, the products of a godless occidental education, ignorant of the sublime principles and lofty ideals of the faith they nominally profess to follow, and poisoned by its calumniation by malicious critics, are unable to assess its intrinsic merit and to appreciate its inestimable beauty.

It is a happy augury, however, that signs of renaissance are visible all over the Muslim world. It may be hoped that the revival of true Islam, the pristine character of which is still unimpaired, will not be long in coming. May God grant good sense to the Muslims of different sects to realise the gravity of the situation and enable them to save Islam from disruption by tiding over the crisis through which it is passing.

Toleration in Islam

It is nothing but travesty of truth to say that Islam is an intolerant religion. In an age of extreme religious intolerance, it was the Prophet of Islam who, for the first time in the history of the world, not only enunciated and preached the principle of "no compulsion in religion," but also constantly practised it himself. He strictly prohibited forcible conversion, proclaiming, "La ikraha fiddin," (let there be no compulsion in religion). He treated the pious Jews and Christians with great respect and courtesy. It is on record that once he accommodated in his own mosque a Christian deputation from Najran,—a practcal illustration of the treatment of non-Muslims as friends and brothers, worthy to occupy even the sacred mosque as honoured guests. Thus he showed in various ways that he strongly disapproved of all kinds of religious intolerance.

In fact Islam allows perfect freedom of conscience, respects difference of opinion in religious matters, protects the life and property of the followers of other religions just as it does of the Muslims, and is thus unmistakably a religion of tolerance. Under Quranic injunction the Muslims are assured that "no soul can believe without the permission of God," and they have to say to non-Muslims, "unto you your religion and unto me my religion." "If your Lord had pleased surely all those who are in the earth would have believed, all of them; will you then force men till they become believers". Al-Quran.

The Prophet of Islam entered into treaties with several Christian tribes promising them his protection and guaranteeing them the free exercise of their religion and to their clergy the undisturbed enjoyment of all their rights and authority. Hazrat Ali, the fourth Khalifa, particularly enjoined the protection of the rights of the "Zimmes" (non-Muslim citizens) in his testament to Hazrat Hossain, the great martyr of Kerbala. He said, "Their life is my life, their blood is my blood and their honour is my honour. See that none ill-treats them, for they are your 'Zimma', responsibility from God."

Is not the existence of so many sects of Christians in countries that were for centuries under Muslim rule an abiding testimony to the great toleration they enjoyed? If some of them sometimes suffered persecution at the hands of bigots or fanatics, it must have been due to some exceptional local circumstance, and not to any settled principle of intolerance.

It would not have been at all difficult for the powerful Muslim rulers to sweep away Christianity from their dominions as Ferdinand and Isabella drove Islam out of Spain, or Louis XIV made Protestantism penal in France, or the Jews were kept out of England for three centuries and a half. The very survival of the Eastern Churches in Asia, that were entirely cut off from communication with the rest of Christendom, is a very strong proof of the tolerant attitude of Muslim Governments towards them. The history of Islam has not recorded any instance of cruel persecution such as that of Hypatia or Bruno or Galileo. Its pages have not been soiled by anything like the records of terrible inquisitions instituted by the Popes and potentates of Europe. In fact, the early Muslims set an example of tolerance towards the non-Muslims, particularly the Jews and the Christians, who enjoyed a measure of toleration the like of which was not to be found anywhere in the world until quite modern times.

The Khalifas and other Muslim rulers, by their considerate treatment of non-Muslims, showed how tolerant a religion Islam is. When Jerusalem submitted to Khalifa Omar, he granted to all its inhabitants "security for their lives, their possessions, their churches, their crosses and all that concerns their religion". He further stipulated that their "churches shall not be changed into dwelling-places, nor destroyed, neither shall they nor their appurtenances be in any way diminished, nor shall any constraint be put upon them in the matter of their faith, nor shall any one of them be harmed". In complete contrast to this the crusaders, when Jerusalem fell into their hands after the defeat of the Muslims in 1039 A.D., massacred 70,000 Muslims, men, women and helpless children.

One of the first steps taken by Muhammad II, after the capture of Constantinople, was to secure the allegiance of its Christian inhabitants by proclaiming himself the protector of the Greek Church. Persecution of the Christians was most strictly forbidden; a decree was granted to the newly-elected patriarch which secured to him and his successors the enjoyment of all the old privileges, revenues and exemptions enjoyed under the former ruler. This reconciled the Greeks to the change of masters and led them to prefer the domination of the Sultan to that of any Christian power.

"The treatment of their Christian subjects," writes Arnold, "by the Ottoman emperors—at least for two centuries after their conquest of Greece—exhibits a toleration such as was at that time quite unknown in the rest of Europe. The Calvinists of Hungary and Transylvania and the Unitarians of the latter country long preferred to submit to the Turks rather than fall into the hands of the fanatical House of Hapsburg . . . . It was to Turkey that the persecuted Spanish Jews fled for refuge in enormous numbers to the end of the fifteenth century, and the Cossacks who belonged to the sect of the Old Believers and were persecuted by the Russian State Church, found in the dominions of the Sultan the toleration which their Christian brethern denied them".

While thus the Christians of different sects were quite safe under the Turks, who never compelled any one to renounce his faith, the Catholic Poles inflicted horrible atrocities on the Russians of the Orthodox Eastern Church. In the course of about fifty years they are said to have put to death seventy to eighty thousand souls—nuns, women, girls, boys and infant children. It was the unexampled tolerance of the Muslims that induced Macarinus, Patriarch of Antioch in the seventeenth century, to say, "God perpetuate the empire of the Turks for ever and ever for they take their impost and enter into no account of religion, be their subjects Christians, Nazarenes, Jews or Samarians."

The history of Spain under Muslim rule for about eight hundred years (711 to 1502) is singularly free from persecution. In fact, the toleration shown towards their Christian subjects by the Muslim rulers of Spain and the freedom of intercourse between the followers of the two religions brought about a certain amount of assimilation in the two communities and inter-marriage between them became frequent. What happened when Spain was recaptured by the Christians in 1502 A.D.? Ferdinand and Isabella issued an edict forbidding the professing of Islam throughout the kingdom. The result was that those who were not in a position to quit Spain were either converted to Christianity or put to death. Similar edicts of a brutally severe character were passed by Christian Governments against the Jews who refused to be baptised. They consequently hailed the Muslims as their deliverers.

In connection with the question of intolerance by the Muslim sovereigns, much has been made of the tax known as Jaziah. But it does not seem to be generally known that it was a tax imposed only on those whose religious scruples precluded them from serving in the army, in return for the protection secured for them by the arms of the Muslims. This tax was to have been paid on the distinct condition that the assessees would be protected from oppression by Muslims or others. It was stated in the treaties, "If we protect you, then Jaziah is due to us, but if we do not, then it is not due." As a rule it was levied on the able-bodied men in lieu of the military service they would have been called upon to perform had they been Muslims. When any non-Muslim people served in the Muslim army they were exempted from the payment of Jaziah.

The allegation of persecution of their non-Muslim subjects, as a rule, by the Muslim rulers of India has no foundation in fact. Most of the powerful Muslim emperors and kings entrusted to non-Muslims the most responsible offices, both civil and military, and substantially contributed for the maintenance of their temples and priests. Perhaps it is not known to many that the Biswanath Mandir at Benares and the Bishnupad Mandir at Gaya, among many other Hindu places of worship, are still maintained out of the income of properties granted by these much-abused Muslim rulers.

Islam is perhaps the only great religion that has sanctioned inter-dining and inter-marriage among the followers of different faiths. A Muslim may dine with a Jew or a Christian and may marry a Jewsih or Christian female and leave her free to follow her own faith. As according to Islam all true religions had their origin in divine revelation, there can be nothing un-Islamic in giving freedom of conscience to such a wife by a Muslim husband. The opposite arrangement could not be sanctioned as a Muslim woman cannot enjoy such freedom of conscience and rights and privileges in a non-Muslim household. This is an instance of religious toleration unique in the history of mankind. No other religion tolerates such close association of its followers with the followers of a different faith.

CHAPTER III

HOW ISLAM WAS PROPAGATED

History bears incontestible testimony to the fact that Islam was propagated by preaching and persuasion; its simplicity, sublimity and practicability having made a most effective appeal to all classes of people who came in contact with it. What can be a more convincing proof of this than the fact that even savage infidel conquerors of Muslim countries had to succumb to Islam's irresistible spiritual force? In the eleventh century of the Christian era, barbarous Selijuk Turks, and in the thirteenth century ferocious Mongol hordes under Chengiz Khan ravaged some of the most advanced Muslim kingdoms, burning, massacring and laying the country waste. "There is no event in the history of Islam" writes T. W. Arnold "that for terror and desolation can be compared to the Mongol conquest. Like an avalanche, the hosts of Chengiz Khan swept over the centres of Muslim culture and civilisation, leaving behind bare deserts and shapeless ruins where before had stood the palaces of stately cities, girt about with gardens and fruitful corn land . . . History has nothing to relate that at all approaches it." In the city of Herat only 40 persons are said to have escaped out of 100,000. Is it not most amazing that even such ferocious savages could be won over by the Muslim missionaries? The primitive religion of the Mongols was Shamanism, which says Arnold "could not long withstand the efforts of a proselytising faith, possessed of a systematic theology, capable of satisfying the demands of reason . . . . When once the Mongols had been brought into contact with civilised races, they responded to their civilising influences." Buddhists, Christians and Muslims entered into rivalry with one another for the conversion of their conquerors. The Muslims, however, were successful; they gradually won over to their faith the savages who had destroyed their centres of culture. Impressed by the intrinsic beauties of Islam they could not help embracing it. History cannot cite another instance of conquerors accepting the religion of the conquered.

There is no record that Muslims ever undertook any crusade for the sake of spreading their religion. Their conquests were all business propositions for defence and colonisation purposes; they fought non-Muslims for domination over them, not for compelling them to renounce their faith. In refuting the oft-repeated allegation that Islam was propagated by force, 'with the sword in one hand and the

Quran in the other,' Mahtama Gandhi very truly said "it was not the sword that won a place for Islam in the scheme of life." Altogether unaided by temporal powers, Muslim missionaries carried their faith right into the hearts of Central Africa, China, the East India Islands, Japan, Australia, Europe and America.

The Prophets and patriarchs of old had sanctioned the use of arms for the sake of religion. Their followers felt no hesitation in unsheathing the sword for indiscriminate slaughter of their religious opponents. The terrible massacre of and by the Jews and the Christians in European countries are historical events too well-known to need detailed description. It was the Prophet of Islam who for the first time in the history of the world put a check on such abuse of arms by strictly restricting their use to defensive and colonisation purposes, absolutely forbidding any "compulsion in religion".

The Muslims were permitted to have recourse to arms for defensive purposes and not offensive, and it was based on three grounds. (1) To oppose and expel those that attacked the Muslims without any just cause. The right of self-defence is allowed by all nations and all laws.

(2) The Muslims had been exiled from their homes and all their properties were seized on no

other ground than that they believed Allah to be their sole Lord. (3) The third ground was the protection and preservation of all places wherein Allah's name is much remembered, be they Christian cloisters and churches, the synagogues of the Jews or the mosques of the Muslims. Thus the wars that the Prophet of Islam waged were defensive wars. In fact, conversion was not the aim of any Muslim war. The chief object of *Jihad*, of which so much has been made by Islam's opponents, is the protection of Muslims and of their mosques and other places of worship.

Of the six great religions of the world three, namely, Buddhism, Christianity and Islam are missionary religions, while Hinduism, Judaism and Zoroastrianism are non-missionary religions. From its very inception Islam has been a missionary religion both in theory and practice. Every simple untaught Muslim may be said to be a missionary of his religion. The trader combines proselytism with the sale of his merchandise. Even a prisoner tries to convert his non-Muslim fellow-prisoners. Thus the Muslims carried with them the message of Islam to every land they penetrated and their proselytising efforts were generally successful everywhere.

The census report published by the League of Nations gives the latest figures for the total population of the followers of different religions. According to this report the total population of the Islamic world is about 603 millions, that is about one-third of the whole human race. The countries that contain the largest number of Muslims were not conquered by the Muslim armies but by the Muslim missionaries, as will appear from the following table which gives the census of Muslims in various parts of the globe :—

Countries.	Number of Muslims.
North Africa ...	294,680,000
Middle and South Africa ...	9,280,000
East Africa	9,257,000
Eastern Europe ...	7,102,000
Soviet Russia ...	12,225,000
Middle and East Asia ...	31,830,000
India (including tribal area)	89,118,504
Malaya	3,034,092
China	40,800,000
Java and the neighbouring Island ...	95,985,000
Other countries ...	10,803
	603,322,399

The above table does not contain the number of Muslims in South America where Islam is rapidly spreading, although there is no Muslim monarch there.

The following list, taken from the recent report published by the Christian Missionary Society, gives the number of Muslims in different places in South America :—

	Countries.	Number of Muslims.
1.	Argentine ...	... 9,520
2.	Brazil ...	... 111,700
3.	Bergdey ...	 7,000
4.	Chile ...	... 150
5.	Cuba ...	... 3,000
6.	Dutch Guiana	... 20,314
7.	French Guiana	... 1,617
8.	Guadoupe ...	... 3,000
9.	Jamaica ...	... 3,403
10.	Martiniquedel	... 2,000
11.	British Guiana	... 1,536
12.	Peru ...	... 6,000
13.	Trinidad ...	... 111,493
14.	Windward Islands	... 300

The history of Islam in Africa covers a period of well-nigh thirteen centuries and embraces two-thirds of this vast continent. The Muslim conquerors showed great zeal for the progress of Islam, which was propagated solely by force of persuasion.

From the sixth century there was a considerable trade between China and Arabia by way of Ceylon, and by the middle of the eighth century Arab traders were to be found in large numbers in Canton. It was these traders who introduced Islam into China. The Province of Yunan has the largest number of Muslims in China. At the beginning of the fourteenth century all the inhabitants of its capital, Talifu, are said to have been Muslims. The Chinese Government has always given to its Muslim subjects the same privileges as are enjoyed by the rest of the population. No office of State is closed to them. Muslim governors of provinces, ministers of state, generals and magistrates have always enjoyed the confidence and respect both of the rulers and the people.

The history of Java, Malaya and the neighbouring Islands, during the last six hundred years furnishes one of the most interesting chapters in the story of the spread of Islam by missionary efforts. Next to Africa they have the largest number of Muslims in the world. As observed by Stoddard, "the amazing success of Islam was due to the character of the Arab race and the nature of Muhammad's teachings". The heathen inhabitants were greatly impressed by the sublime teachings of Islam as well as by the devout behaviour and superior culture of the Muslims.

In India also force played no part in the conversion of the Hindus. With few exceptions the kings of the Pathan dynasties and the Mughal emperors, as a rule, displayed very little zeal for proselytism. This is evident from the preponderance of Hindu population even at the centres of Muslim power. It was in East Bengal and Southern India, and not in the Punjab, North-Western Provinces, Oudh or Bihar, where the Muslim power was at its height, that the peaceful Muslim missionaries achieved their greatest triumph; their teaching, persuasion and ideal life being the only influences at work. As far as number is concerned, the missionaries were most successful in Eastern Bengal, where "to the teeming low castes" writes Sir W. W. Hunter "who had sat for ages abject on the outermost pale of the Hindu community, was offered entrance into a new social organisation," in which there was no question of untouchability.

Had Islam been propagated in India by the sword, perhaps there would not have been left even a single non-Muslim in some places, particularly in the neighbourhood of the seats of Muslim Government. But where do Muslims preponderate in

India? Not in Delhi, or in Agra or in Lucknow, where an overwhelming majority of the population continue to be Hindu in spite of seven hundred years of Muslim rule, but in Sylhet, in Chittagong, in Noakhali, far away from the capital cities, where saints and sages like Shah Jalal and Bajid Bostani, spread Islam by the use of the tongue, not by the use of the sword, by preaching and persuasion, not by force and compulsion.

---

*

*

CHAPTER IV.

HAZRAT MUHAMMAD AS A SOCIAL REFORMER

Hazrat Muhammad was the greatest social reformer the world has ever produced. Even if he had not been a religious reformer, his name would have found a prominent and permanent place in world history as a social reformer. It is one thing to promulgate a new faith, which mainly concerns individuals and though professed by them might not really be practised, but it is quite a different thing to attack and upset the whole fabric of a social organisation, provoking bitter opposition from a whole nation consisting of millions of individuals. Before Hazrat Muhammad's advent, Arabia, nay the whole of the known world, was steeped in vice, superstition and barbarism. The Arabs were wild savages, and social inequality, down-trodden womanhood, slavery, drunkenness, debauchery, gambling, rapacity, blood-thirstiness and such other heinous vices were rampant among them. No prophet before Hazrat Muhammad seems to have thought of tackling these horrible evils. He ruthlessly attacked them one after another and totally crushed them in no time, to the immense relief of humanity. Thus within a short time were the barbarous and impious Arabs transformed into a civilised and religious nation.

Equality of Man

Of all the social reforms initiated by Hazrat Muhammad the removal of inequality among human beings was the most beneficial and far-reaching in consequences. He found no reason for any distinction between man and man on account of mere accident of birth in a particular family or particular profession or particular country. So he scrupulously broke down all artificial barriers which society had set up to fortify privileges of wealth or work or colour or country. All human beings, he declared, were equal, and the highest rank was his who was the most obedient to God and most useful to mankind. Hazrat Muhammad thus established a universal brotherhood of man under the Fatherhood of God, welding high and low, rich and poor, white and black into one common fraternity. As soon as the lowest of the low, say a sweeper, or the blackest of the black, say a Negro, embraced Islam, he was entitled to say prayers in the same place, to drink water from the same cup and to take food from the same dish as a Muslim of the highest rank.

The conception of human brotherhood that transcends geographical and racial boundaries is unrealised in other great religions of the world. It is Islam alone that "rules out in theory, no less than in practice, the claims of race or nation, caste or colour, to break the unity or to mar the harmony of the human family". In fact it recognises no distinction other than that of intentions and acts. "God does not look at your lineage or faces," says the Prophet, "but He looks into your hearts...he among you that is most favoured of Allah is the one that is most pious". The institution of Islam, step by step, worked towards the ideal of a universal brotherhood of man. They laid the basis of a society in which all men and women, to whatever nation or caste they belonged, whatever their profession or rank, had equal rights and privileges.

The object Hazrat Muhammad had in view was to bring the whole of humanity on one common platform as one class, one community and one nation, having the same ideals and sharing the same privileges, so that there might not be any question of superiority and inferiority, of birth and family, of rank and race. This absolute equality impelled all Muslims, irrespective of their position in life, to exert themselves in all spheres of human activities. No one before Hazrat Muhammad had ever conceived any idea of such a practical world-wide brotherhood.

Islamic brotherhood is not merely a verbal concept; it is an undisputed fact. Once admitted into the fold of Islam any human being, however low his position might have been before his conversion, becomes the proud possessor of all the rights and privileges that a Muslim of the highest rank is entitled to claim. A death-knell to all superiority and inferiority, based on rigid social distinction, has thus been sounded. The lowest among the believers can claim equality with the highest; there is no depressed class or untouchability.

It is this genuine spirit of brotherhood infused by Islam into the heterogenous units of humanity, at war with one another, that ushered in a new era of peace and good-will in the world in those troublous times. The entire humanity was, as it were, bound together, man to man, nation to nation, state to state. "If Islam had done nothing else except eliminating, as it has incontestably done, the barriers of racial antipathy and national exclusiveness among one-fifth of mankind, scattered over the surface of the globe and covering almost every land and clime, even then civilisation would have been immensely indebted to it for ever"

In a mosque, at the time of congregational prayers, the unique imposing sight which one sees is altogether unknown and unimaginable anywhere else on the globe. There all meet on the same platform in sincere remembrance of their Creator and there sit side by side or stand shoulder to shoulder the prince and the peasant, the potentate and the pauper, the servant and the master, the black and the white, the Arab and the Abyssinian, irrespective of any distinction of blood or colour, wealth or learning and without any precedence whatsoever; and when they prostrate in prayer the head of the prince touches the feet of the peasant if the latter happens to be in the preceding row. No Muslim, however low his position, is debarred from entrance into a mosque or denied a seat in the first row. In a moqsue there are no rented pews or spęcial reserved seats, as in a church. The ex-king Amanullah, in the palmy days of his rule in Afghanistan, being almost always the last to join the congregation, could get no better place than that behind the hindmost row, the one generally reserved for keeping shoes. To those who would try to find a better place for him he would say, "I am no better than you are". Islam recognises only one distinction. This is the real message and true spirit of the teachings of Islam. In fact there is no other aristocracy that

Islam has sanctioned. Does this not unmistakably prove that Islam has broken down all man-made barriers of distinction and all prejudices of race and colour?

The Haj (Islamic pilgrimage to Holy Mecca) is the one unique spiritual gathering in the world, which most effectively demonstrates how we are all perfectly equal in the eyes of God. Even clothes, the last vestige of distinction, are discarded, and all, dressed in the same two white unsewn pieces of linen, gather in and around the Sacred House of Kaaba and exclaim with one voice while circumambulating it: "Here I am at Thy service, my Lord".

No Islamic injunction is without some deep significance. The Muslims have been enjoined to say their prayers in congregation as often as they can, once or twice a day, if not five times, in larger congregation once a week, in a still larger congregation twice a year and in a congregation of the Muslims of the whole world at least once in life,—and it has been laid down that congregational prayers are far more meritorious than prayers offered alone. Finding that I could better concentrate my mind and could have deeper meditation when alone in a solitary place than with others in a mosque, I set about thinking as to the wisdom and utility of congregational prayers. It struck me that there are many purposes, religious, social, political and humanitarian, in this injunction. The first of these is the practical illustration of two of the most essential features of Islam—humility before God and equality among men. This can hardly be better illustrated than by prostration before God in a public place, giving precedence to one's inferior in rank and wealth.

A congregation for prayers further teaches most effectively, though imperceptibly, how order and discipline, so very necessary for all human affairs, both in peace and war, are to be maintained in an assemblage, and how commands given by the leader have to be promptly obeyed. A highly-placed European who had occasion to witness one such congregation, remarked that thousands of people standing together in pin-drop silence and going down on their knees and then to the ground all together at one word from the man at the head, was the most amazing sight he had ever seen in any country.

Moreover, a congregation for prayers is intended to bring the Muslims together, as frequently as possible, for exchange of thoughts and ideas, for discussion of religious, social and political matters, for devising means for meeting the moral and material requirements of the people. During the

Prophet's time, the mosque was not merely a place of worship, as it is now, but the Muslim's council chamber, the court house, the war office, the town hall, the school building, even the guest house. The present-day Muslims seem to have forgotten all this. They now generally go to the mosque like strangers, sit there like strangers, and depart like strangers, hardly a word passing among many of them. Few of the Muslims, not to speak of non-Muslims, realise now-a-days the real significance and intended purpose of the lofty injunctions of the Quran. Islam now-a-days seems to lie buried under rites and rituals, forms and formulas, terms and trappings, the slightest deviation from which calls forth severe condemnation from people who, of all others, ought to have known what true Islam is.

Slavery

Manumission of slaves was the natural consequence of the declaration of the equality of man. Slavery was in vogue among all nations of antiquity. The Greeks, the Romans, the Jews, the Christians, all had slaves whom they treated most inhumanly, possessing the power of life and death over them. Marriage between slaves was not legal, and between the slaves and the free, marriage was prohibited under frightful penalties. If a free woman married a slave, she was to be put to death and the slave burnt alive. Thus the slaves had perpetually to live a life of unmitigated drudgery in the service of their pitiless masters. Such was the miserable lot of the slaves until Hazrat Muhammad came to their rescue.

Christianity adopted slavery as a recognised institution, "a constitution of nature", and did nothing to mitigate its baneful character or to improve the status of slaves. In fact during the seventeenth and part of the eighteenth century even the Puritan Englishmen possessed large slave colonies, and Christian divines racked their brains to devise apologies and invent religious justification for slave-driving. After the massacre of Drogheda by Cromwell and the suppression of the insurrection in Ireland, the English Protestants sold wholesale the Irish men and women to the colonists in Virginia, Pennsylvania and other places. The same was done after Monmouth's rebellion.

Islam, far from consecrating slavery, as has been maliciously affirmed by its unjust critics, provided in every feasible way for its abolition and extinction by circumscribing the means of possession. It strongly condemned slavery and strictly forbade the enslavement of Muslims. Hazrat Muhammad did all that was possible to raise the status of the slaves. He emphatically declared that there was no act more acceptable to God than the enfranchisement of slaves. He would purchase slaves only to see them free. He repeatedly exhorted his followers in the name of God to treat the slaves with kindness and justice. "And as to your slaves, see that ye feed them as ye feed yourselves and clothe them as ye clothe yourselves". Once a follower enquired of him what was most acceptable to God and he promptly replied "setting free of slaves". In fact for many social and religious derelictions freeing of slaves was the only penance prescribed by Islam.

Among Muslims a slave today may be a king tomorrow. He may become the head of a most respectable family by marrying his master's daughter after loyal and devoted service to his master for some time. Muslim slaves ruled kingdoms and founded royal dynasties. Subuktegin, the founder of the Ghuznavi dynasty, Kutbuddin, the first Muslim King of Delhi, Balban who efficiently ruled India for about half a century, were all slaves. Is there any instance of such treatment of slaves in the world's history?

Status of Woman in Islam

Another most beneficial reform effected by the Holy Prophet of Arabia was the amelioration of the condition of the female sex. No religion before Islam did anything, worth mentioning, to improve woman's position. It was Islam that for the first time vindicated woman's rights and raised her to the level which she was entitled to occupy as mother, sister and partner of man. In fact the improvement that Islam brought about in the position of woman was unparalleled in the history of mankind. It gave her a status unknown and unthought-of before, and unsurpassed even to this day after fourteen hundred years.

In pre-Islamic days woman was no better than a chattel, intended for the gratification of man. In all countries known as civilised in ancient times—Greece, Rome, Egypt, Persia and China—man's estimate of woman was so low that it is beyond conception in the twentieth century. She was looked down upon on account of her supposed intellectual inferiority, her only function being the management of the household and the procreation of children. Nowhere in the world did she get the treatment she was entitled to as man's partner in life. Even among the Athenians, the most cultured and civilised of all nations of antiquity, the wife was the slave of every caprice and whim of her husband; she was a mere chattel, marketable and transferable to others at the sweet will of the head of the family. Personal rights she had none, she was precluded from all share in the property of her father as well as of her husband.

No Prophet before Hazrat Muhammad was moved by the miseries and disabilities of half the human race. Far from doing anything for the elevation of woman, other Prophets had perpetuated by their sanction the disabilities imposed upon her by the selfishness of man. The followers of some of them regarded her as "the gate of the devil," "the road to iniquity", "the poison of the asp", "the instrument which the devil uses to gain possession of our soul." The Biblical injunction to the wife was: "Thy desire shall be to thy husband and he shall rule over thee." The legal position of woman in most advanced countries of Christendom even now compares most unfavourably with that of a Muslim woman. Until very recently a married woman even in civilised England possessed no rights independently of her husband, although by courtesy called his "better half." It is only recently that the position of woman in England has been improved by some legislative enactments.

Islam secured to woman such rights and privileges as she had never enjoyed before. She was placed on a footing of perfect equality with man in the exercise of all legal powers and functions. In the matter of inheritance and individual right of property, the position of a Muslim woman is far better than that of women professing any other religion. "Men ought to have a part of what their parents and kindred leave", says the Quran, "and women a part of what their parents and kindred leave; let them have a stated share." Thus, fourteen hundred years ago, Islam gave woman the right to property. But she did not get that right in England until 1875, and she has not got it in France even yet.

A Muslim woman has the full right of enjoying and alienating her property. She can do business independently and enter into any contract she likes; her husband has no right of interference. After marriage she retains her distinct individuality and she has not to assume her husband's name as Mrs. So & So. Thus she is an independent co-sharer and a true partner of man.

As regards marriage, a Muslim woman has been given full liberty in the choice of her husband. No contract is valid without her consent; she has first to declare her consent, man merely accepts her offer. No guardian can give his major female ward in marriage without first obtaining her consent. If married by the guardian in her minority, she can repudiate the marriage on attaining majority.

Besides, no marriage contract is complete without the settlement of a dowry for the wife. Her claim to it, on the death of her husband, has preference over all creditors and heirs to the property of the deceased. As regards divorce, the woman also has the right to divorce the man under certain circumstances.

According to the Quran, woman has as much capacity for intellectual and spiritual progress as man. In her honour one complete chapter of the Quran has been revealed after her name. The very first verse of this chapter strikes the key-note: "O people, fear your Lord, who hath created you from one soul, and of his kind created his wife and from these hath spread abroad many men and women. And fear your God, in whose name ye ask mutual favour, and reverence the woman that bear you. Verily God is watching you."

Does this not give the lie direct to the monstrous allegation made by some non-Muslim writers that Islam recognises no soul in woman? The Quran does not even hold, as does the Bible, that woman was made for man. On the contrary, it distinctly teaches that each has obligations towards the other on an equal basis. "And if you men have certain rights on them (women), they have similar rights on you in all fairness"

The Prophet of Islam enforced respect for woman as one of the essential teachings of his creed. He symbolically placed Paradise at the feet of the mother, and declared that "woman is sovereign in the house of her husband." The ideal of wifehood in Islam is love and affection and not subordination and subservience. The Muslims regard woman as a safeguard against sin, and not "the road to iniquity"; as a strong fortress against the inroads of Satan and not "the gate of the devil"; as a lighthouse of virtue that saves man from moral shipwreck when tossed by the raging waves of passion, and not "the instrument which the devil uses to gain possession of our souls." To a Muslim it is the pure love of a virtuous woman that transforms the brute of a man into an angelic being.

Such is the exalted position to which Islam raised womankind. Their position in Muslim countries is infinitely better in certain respects than that of their sisters in other countries. If in some places Muslim women are backward in education and enlightenment and do not occupy their proper place in society or even in their homes, it is due to lack of culture in the community, and not to any flaw in Islamic laws or tenets. It would be doing a great injustice to Islam to judge it by the life led by many of its present-day followers.

"The Teacher," truly observes Syed Amir Ali, "who in an age when no country, no system, no community gave any right to woman, maiden or married, mother or wife, who in a country where the birth of a daughter was considered a calamity, secured to the sex rights which are only unwillingly and under pressure being conceded to them by the civilised nations in the twentieth century, deserves the gratitude of humanity. If Muhammad had done nothing more, his claim to be a benefactor of mankind would still have been indisputable".

Polygamy

In connection with woman's status in Islam a word about polygamy may not be out of place. The impression prevailing among some people that Islam has instituted polygamy and a Muslim has to marry a number of wives is absolutely incorrect. The marrying of more than one wife by a Muslim is permissive and not binding, and the conditional permission is coupled with such restrictions that in effect it amounts almost to a prohibition.

Besides immensely raising the social and legal status of woman, the Prophet of Islam did much to minimise her domestic and conjugal hardships. Polygamy originated, like polyandry, out of sheer necessity on account of the preponderance of females and dearth of males caused by frequent tribal wars and clannish quarrels and tragedies of hunting and barbaric life. In course of time it came to be regarded as a recognised institution among all eastern nations of antiquity, and it continued even when the necessity of saving women from destitution and starvation had ceased. Besides, its practice by prophets and patriarchs of old was believed to have given it a religions sanction. The Bible does not prohibit polygamy. It was the Nicene council of 320 A.D. that advocated monogamy. But the prohibitory laws of the Christian empire failed to stop polygamy, and merely drove the evil custom into morganatic and underground channels.

By the time Islam was promulgated, polygamy had attained such an enormous universality that there was no limit to the number of wives and concubines an Arab, or for the matter of that most ancient people, might have. In fact the Arabs knew not what sexual morality was, and even the guardian sometimes outraged their wards, and the son of a deceased man included in his harem his step-mothers. In such a horrible state of things it would have been impossible to put down polgamy all at once by an injunction for total prohibition. Steps had, therefore, to be taken for the gradual eradication of the evil by limiting the number of contemporanious marriages and by making absolute equity towards all co-wives obligatory on he male. This was meant to signify equality of treatment not merely in the matter of domestic requirements, such as diet, lodging, clothing, but also complete equity in love and treatment. Thus it was an indirect prohibition, absolute justice in matters of sentiment and conjugal dealings being next to impossible.

The Quran has prescribed monogamy as the rule and polygamy as an exception to be contracted only in certain abnormal circumstances. The Quranic permission must not be taken as an injunction or even as an encouragement. It distinctly lays down : "If you feel you cannot do justice between them, then marry only one." Besides, the ordinances of a practical religion should be such as may be worked out in actual life. Contingent cases, such as barrenness, wreck of health, a wife's turning a virago, had to be provided for. Restrained and regulated polygamy is perhaps a good protector of female chastity. It is not altogether unnatural that prostitution and polyandry with consequent abortion and infanticide, should prevail where polygamy is not permitted under any circumstance.

Canon Isaac Taylor truly observed in the course of his address to the Church Congress, "The strictly-regulated polygamy of Muslim lands is infinitely less degrading to women and less injurious to men than the promiscuous polyandry which is the curse of Christian cities and which is absolutely unknown in Islam."

In respect of matrimony, Hazrat Muhammad did not imitate his predecessors. David, "the man after God's heart," had hundreds of wives and Moses and other prophets had many more than one. But Hazrat Muhammad was a bachelor up to the age of twenty-five and he was held in high esteem for his pious nature and pure character. In his twenty-fifth year he married a widow fifteen years his senior in age and lived very happily with her for another twenty-five years, "loving her truly and her alone". After her death, in his fifty-first year when "the heat of his years" (says Carlyle) "was gone, the prurient heat of his life all burnt out," he married Ayesha, the only virgin he ever took to wife. She was the daughter of his bosom friend and constant companion, Hazrat Abu Bakr, the first male convert to his faith and its most enthusiastic supporter. At a still more advanced age he had to take under his protection, by joining in wedlock, some helpless widows, whose husbands had fallen in Islam's battles or had otherwise made immense sacrifices for its cause.

Among advanced Muslims of the present day plurality of wives is now regarded as a great evil, and the exceptional permission is believed to have been temporary under certain social or physically unavoidable circumstances. Steps are being taken in Turkey and elsewhere to put it down. It is hoped that, before long, polygamy will totally disappear from Muslim countries.

Drunkenness

Unrestricted indulgence in intoxicating liquors was one of the chief features of pre-Islamic Arab society. But one single command of Hazrat Muhammad was enough to wean the whole nation from this pernicious evil in an incredibly short time. "O you who believe! intoxicants and games of chance are unclean—the devil's work: shun it therefore, that you may be successful. The devil only desires to cause enmity and hatred to spring in your midst by means of intoxicants and games of chance, and to keep you off from the remembrance of Allah and from prayer: will you then desist." Al Quran. Hardly had these words come out of the Prophet's lips when the very jars in which liquors were made and stored, were broken to pieces and the streets of Medina flowed with streams of wine. Since then during these fourteen hundred years Muslim brotherhood has been the most notable total abstinence association in the globe, and the 'dryness' of Muslim countries and the sobriety of the bulk of their population have been a wonder of the world. Can history present another instance of so wonderful a transformation, brought about so easily, yet so thoroughly, so effectively, so permannently?

Drunkenness has all along been a curse of Christian countries. According to the Bible, wine is a sacred thing, which is used in the Sacrament. The pernicious effect of alcoholic liquors on man's health has, however, been at last realised in this twentieth century and campaigns of teetotalism have been started. But the evil of drinking has got such a firm hold on Christian countries that it has been found to be impossible to put a stop to it. America, which is now-a-days more forward in such movements than other countries, led a crusade against the evil and tried to make the country "dry" by legislation. The experiment, however, has proved a total failure. Drastic legislative and administrative measures, costing millions of dollars, have failed to drive drinking out of Christian America. The laws that were passed for the purpose have been repealed and the country has again been given up to the demon of drink.

Charity and Capitalism

One of the religious ordinances for the Muslims is *Zakat* or charity. Other religions have also enjoined charity, but none of them prescribed its form or extent. Neither the Bible nor any other scripture so definitely defined it as did the Quran. It has been laid down in the Quran that every Muslim must pay annually 2½ per cent. of his possessions in cash or gold and a proportionate share of other possessions as *Zakat* for the benefit of the needy—the poor who cannot maintain themselves, debtors who have not the means to repay, slaves so that they can buy their own freedom, travellers and strangers who have no passage money. Besides *Zakat,* every head of a family has to pay, on the occasion of the Eid on the expiry of the fasting month of Ramzan, a certain fixed sum, known as *Fitra,* towards charity for himself and for every one of his dependents.

Islam does not favour capitalism—amassing of wealth in the hands of particular individuals. It has done much to equalise the worldly conditions of people. Besides the institution of *Zakat* and *Fitra,* it adopted other means for the equitable distribution of wealth. There is no law of primogeniture in Islam. The Islamic law of inheritance distributes a deceased person's estate proportionately among his widow and his sons and daughters, the sons getting double of the daughters, without preference to any one of them by reason of priority or age.

Usury is strictly forbidden by Islam. The debtor has to return only the principal to the creditor. Exploitation of any one's personal need for another's profit is very severely condemned by Islam.

Thus of all religions Islam alone adopted several means to minimise the evils of capitalism.

Personal Hygiene

Islam is perhaps the only religion that has realised the indissoluble connection between the body and the soul. According to it moral and spiritual progress depends also upon personal cleanliness, which, to a Muslim, is next to godliness. It is a necessary preliminary to the adoration of God, Who should be always approached in purity of both body and spirit. A Muslim in addition to bathing, when necessary, has to wash properly five times a day, at the time of ablution before each prayer, those parts of his body that are likely to get soiled in the course of daily work. The Prophet of Islam, who was very particular in matters of personal cleanliness, resented much if a person came to the congregation unclean and with dishevelled hair. He laid particular stress on cleaning of the teeth. "Had I not considered it a great hardship for my followers", he used to say, "I would have made it a *Farz* (an imperative duty) at the time of each prayer". That there was particular significance in this is being realised after thirteen hundred years. The Americans, who are going to be a toothless nation, and other civilised people, have at last realised that sound health depends, to a greater extent, upon keeping the teeth clean than upon anything else and that the root of many a disease from which man suffers, is the unclean tooth. Pyorrhea, caries and similar diseases caused by diseased teeth, due to uncleanliness, perhaps play greater havoc with human health than any other ailment. A high official who had been in poor health for a long time, thought that he was suffering from some serious disease that would at last prove fatal. But when he applied for leave and was called upon to appear before a Medical Board he was told, to his utter surprise, that he had no disease and that all his trouble was due to his teeth having been kept unclean. Another official, who had to appear before a Medical Board under similar circumstances, was told exactly the same thing. The great attention that is being paid now-a-days to the toilet of the teeth and to the science of dentistry unmistakably bears out the significance of the injunction that requires that the teeth should be always kept scrupulously clean.

Similarly other Islamic injunctions regarding personal hygiene are not without some particular purpose. For example, the exhortation regarding the preservation of beard and trimming of moustache has an important hygienic significance. In the scheme of nature there is hardly anything without a purpose. The beard, which symbolises manhood, represents saintliness and stands for gravity, austerity, dignity and holiness, is really intended to protect the face and the throat, and the moustache to serve as a respirator and screen to the nostrils. Dr. Arthur Macdonald of Washington in the course of discussing the fashion of shaving, wrote in the Medical World of Philadelphia, "you might as well shave the fur off the squirrel and cut the feathers from a bird as shave the hair from the face. Just as the hair protects the head so does the beard the face. The moustache is nature's respirator, while the hair covering the jaws and throat gives warmth and protection to the delicate structures under it, especially the fauces and larynx. The hair of the moustache absorbs the miasma and moisture of fogs; the beard takes heat from the warm breath of the mouth as it leaves the chest and supplies it to the cold air taken in. If a man would have increased immunity from toothache, relaxed uvula, coughs, cold, inflammation, disquamation and all the rheums, let him grow a beard . . . . In changeable climates the beard is useful as an equaliser of heat and cold. Shaving appears to render persons more susceptible to violent changes of temperature and consequently more liable to disease. In cold localities the beard is an important defence. The injurious effect of removing this protection, even in midsummer, is shown in huskiness and hoarseness of the voice . . . . The air entering the nose during an hour contains about fourteen hundred organisms of various kinds . . . . the large outside doors, the moustache and beard, which at the very first could stop much of the dust and organisms, are omitted in many cases . . . . "

If it is asked, "what about women"? The answer is "women have not to do so much outdoor work as men and are not, therefore, liable to much exposure. Besides, women, as a rule, have more fat beneath the skin than men have, especially in the neck and the face. The larynx and trachea in woman are deeper seated than in man. Yet notwithstanding these safeguards women are said to have more facial neuralgia than men."

The Prophet of Islam seems to have forestalled the germ theory, long before it was propounded by the medical science. The Muslims were enjoined to grow moustache perhaps with a view to obstruct the passage of the germs in the body through the nostrils. They were further required to clip the moustache short, so that in drinking it might not be dipped into water and thereby facilitate the passage of the germs collected in the moustache into the stomach.

Such is the risk which a beardless and moustacheless man has to run. Yet, it is to be regretted, that the mania for shaving is fast spreading not only among non-Muslims but even among Muslims, in spite of social custom and family tradition and religious exhortation. Would it be too much to expect that what Dr. Macdonald has written would set them athinking?

The founders of the great religions, with the exception of Buddha, were all bearded men—Moses, Jesus, Muhammad. The Greek tragedians and philosophers like Sophocles and Plato were also long-bearded men. Tagore, the representative of Hindu wisdom, is heavily bearded.

The injunction about circumcision also has especial significance. The following remarks on circumcision made by Dr. M. J. Exner M.D., in

"The Rational Sex Life for Men" are well worth quoting in this connection :—

"The frequent cause of persistent nocturnal emissions is a long tight foreskin, causing irritating secretions to gather underneath which the anatomical condition makes it difficult or impossible to remove. They serve to keep the sensitive parts of the penis unduly irritative, a condition which alone is responsible for undermining the health. Under these circumstances circumcision gives prompt relief. With reference to cleanliness and for other important reasons, circumcision of all boys in infancy is desirable".

The Muslims were the pioneers of personal hygiene in Europe. Thomas Oliver, the well-known physician, has truly observed, "Allowing for climatic conditions the most civilised nations are the most washed". This view is opposed to that of the Christian divines. In the rule of the Order of the Temple, St. Bernard laid down that "Knights should be seldom washed and never combed".

Dr. John William Draper writes, "To the Saracens we are indebted for many of our personal comforts. Religiously clean, it was not possible for them to clothe themselves according to the fashion of the natives of Europe, in a garment unchanged till it dropped to pieces of itself, a loathsome mass of vermin, stench and rags . . . . They taught us the use of linen and cotton".

Gustav Diercks says, "As the Muslims came from warm climates, they felt a greater necessity for baths and cleanliness in general, more than the customs of Christians of Europe can show. Consequently the habits of the Muslims were taken up by the Christians and baths were frequently used". So the cleanliness of the present-day Westerners is entirely due to their association with the Saracens of Spain.

Dignity of Labour

The Prophet of Islam impressed on his followers, both by personal example and by precept, the dignity of labour. When a mosque was being built at Medina, he worked like an ordinary labourer, carrying bricks on his head. On one occasion when a respectable person, who could not find any employment, enquired of him what he was to do for the support of his family, he advised him to go to the neighbouring forest with an axe and to cut down wood to sell as fuel. Thus there is no honest work, however low in the estimation of society, that a Muslim should shun, if called upon to do it. In fact on several occasions when beggars came to the door of the Prophet of Islam and he had no cash or food to offer them, he asked them to wait, himself went out to some neighbour who was well off and did some manual work for him and divided the wages of the same between the beggar and his own family.

Punctuality

The debauched and drunken Arabs had hardly any idea of the value of time and the necessity of discipline for a well-ordered society. Early in life the Prophet of Islam realised that if the Arabs were to be organised into a compact nation, they must be under proper control and should know when to act. In promulgating Islam he made such injunctions as would further punctuality and discipline among the Muslims. He prescribed fixed time for the performance of religious duties, particularly the five daily prayers. This was done with a view to impress upon the Muslims the importance of punctuality. Not that prayers said a few minutes earlier or a few minutes later than the appointed time would be unacceptable to God, but the insistence on exact time was intended to remind the Muslims five times a day that they should do their work punctually according to a settled routine, otherwise it might not be properly done.

What can be more regrettable than the fact that in spite of all this insistence on punctuality, the present-day Muslims should have so far forgotten the true significance of the Islamic injunction that their unpunctuality in every-day life seems to be passing into a proverb?

These are some of the important social reforms initiated by Hazrat Muhammad. It would be superfluous to dilate upon the immense good they have done to humanity. Islam brought about the equality of man, elevation of the status of woman, manumission of slaves, suppression of profligacy and drunkenness, advocacy of organised charity, discouragement of capitalism, forbidding of usury, condemnation of exploitation of the poor, commendation of labour, insistence on punctuality, exaltation of marriage and discountenancing of celibacy. But for these reforms, preached and practised since the promulgation of Islam, the progress of human society would have been very much retarded and the condition of mankind would have been altogether different from what it is. For all this an immense debt of the world's gratitude is due to Hazrat Muhammad, who may rightly be styled the greatest social reformer the world has ever produced.

*

CHAPTER V.

HAZRAT MUHAMMAD AS AN EDUCATIONAL REFORMER

Before the advent of Hazrat Muhammad, learning was confined to the few. The priests, anxious to monopolise all power, were opposed to the education of the people in general. Consequently most of the people were ignorant and illiterate. No Messenger of God, from Noah to Jesus, seems to have done anything for the dissemination of knowledge. The Prophet of Islam, though unread himself, was the first to move in this matter. Convinced that the ignorant cannot know God and are unable to realise adequately His goodness and greatness, he made the acquisition of knowledge incumbent upon all his followers, irrespective of sex and rank. "Talabul-Ilme Farizatun Ala Kulle Muslimin Wa Muslimatin" : "Seeking of knowledge is imperative for all Muslims, males and females".

That the Prophet lost no opportunity of laying great stress on the importance of knowledge and of impressing upon his followers the religious necessity of its acquisition, will be conclusively proved by the following quotations from his sayings:—

"A Muslim should study from the cradle to the grave".

"An hour's contemplation and study of God's creation is better than a year's adoration".

"He who leaves home in search of knowledge walks in the path of God".

"Seek knowledge though it be available in China".*

"The ink of the scholar is holier than the blood of the martyr".

"To listen to the words of the learned and to instil into others the lessons of science is better than religious exercises".

"The contemplation of a learned person for one night is more meritorious in the eyes of the Lord than the saying of prayers for several nights".

He who acquires knowledge in the way of the Lord, performs an act of piety; he who speaks of it, praises the Lord; who seeks it, adores God; who dispenses instruction in it, bestows alms; and who

* At the time of the Prophet, China, then under the rule of the great Tang dynasty, was at its zenith in respect of scientific knowledge. The Prophet urged his followers to go in search of knowledge even to such a distant country as China.

imparts it to its fitting objects, performs an act of devotion to God".

"Knowledge enables its possessor to distinguish right from wrong; it lights the way to heaven; it is our friend in the desert, our society in solitude, our companion when friendless; it guides us to happiness; it sustains us in misery; it is an ornament among friends and an armour against enemies".

"Who so pursueth the road of knowledge, Allah will direct him to the road to Paradise; verily the angels spread their arms to receive him who seeketh after knowledge; verily the superiority of a learned man over a mere worshipper is like that of the full moon over the stars".

"He dieth not who takes to learning".

"Whoever reveres the learned reveres me".

Such was the personal teaching of the Prophet, which, for the Muslims, comes next to the Holy Quran. "O Thou who hast knowledge grant knowledge to me", was the constant prayer of the Prophet, who used to tell his followers, "knowledge is the birth-right of the Faithful; they take it wherever they find it".

The Prophet did not approve of his followers being entirely absorbed in the meditation of God, to the exclusion of everything else. He always urged them to acquire knowledge and directed them to go in search of it all over the world, to all peoples. "Four things", he used to say, "support the world: the learning of the wise, the justice of the great, the prayers of the good, and the valour of the brave".

The boundaries of religion were immeasurably enlarged by what the Prophet of Islam taught in respect of knowledge and its acquisition; every branch of learning conducive to human progress came within the purview of Islam. No boundary was set up between sacred and profane knowledge. An insatiable thirst for knowledge was thus created in that dark age, and this gave a tremendous impetus to the development of scientific research in realms hitherto unexplored. As described in my "Islam's Contribution to Science and Civilisation" (*vide* in the Appendix), some undreamt of discoveries and inventions were made, immensely contributing to the progress of civilisation and the welfare of mankind. In fact the early Muslims very largely contributed to the cultural development of the world; there was hardly any important branch of learning of which they did not make themselves masters. "The Arabs", writes Bosworth Smith, "for five hundred years held up the torch of learning to humanity".

*

CHAPTER VI.

NON-MUSLIM OPINION ABOUT ISLAM AND ITS PROPHET

It is an irony of human mentality that Islam, which is the one religion that upholds the truth of all religions and inculcates respect and veneration for all the Messengers of God, should be the most maligned of all religions. Of all the great Prophets of the world Hazrat Muhammad is the nearest and the most reliable historical personage; and yet, strange to say, he is the least understood; and of all the great Revelations granted to mankind, the Quran is the most up-to-date, the most universal and the most many-sided, and yet it is the most misunderstood, and often the most misinterpreted of Scriptures.

It is ignorance and prejudice that seem to have stood in the way of a proper appreciation of Islam and its Prophet. Those who have made a careful study of the Quran, with an unbiassed mind, have not failed to realise its intrinsic worth. Some of the master minds of the West, the great poet Goethe, the great historian Gibbon, the great philosopher

Carlyle, the great socialist George Bernard Shaw, who is regarded as the greatest intellect of the present age, among many others, were profoundly impressed by the message of the Quran. Goethe seems to have fallen into raptures over it: "If Islam be submission to God's will, " he exclaimed, "in Islam we live and die all". Those who have read Carlyle's "The Hero as Prophet" need not be told how highly he appraised the greatness of the Prophet of Islam and his teachings. He was denounced as heathen by his bigoted countrymen and co-religionists, when he emphatically declared Muhammad to be the greatest of Prophets.

George Bernard Shaw, in his characteristic style, has sought to prove that a hundred years hence, and even before it, England in particular, and the rest of the Western world in general, are bound to embrace Islam. Although an atheist himself, and hardly any dogma of any religion has passed unscathed by his trenchant pen, Shaw thinks that Islam is the only religion that will satisfy all intelligent people who want a religion to guide them spiritually, morally and socially. The strongest argument advanced by him to prove the universal acceptability of Islam is that it has great power of absorbing every progress made by philosophy and science. In an interview Mr. Shaw paid the following tribute to the Prophet of Islam :—

"I have always held the religion of Muhammad in high estimation because of its wonderful vitality. It is the only religion which appears to me to possess that assimilating capability to the changing phases of existence which can make itself appeal to every age . . . . The medaeval ecclesiastics either through ignorance or bigotry painted Muhammadanism in the darkest colours. They were in fact trained both to hate the man Muhammad and his religion. To them Muhammad was anti-Christ. I have studied him—the wonderful man—and in my opinion, far from being an anti-Christ he must be called the Saviour of humanity. I believe that if a man like him were to assume the dictatorship of the modern world, he would succeed in solving its problems in a way that would bring it the much-needed peace and happiness. But to proceed: it was in the 19th century that honest thinkers like Carlyle, Goethe and Gibbon perceived intrinsic worth in the religion of Muhammad and thus there was some change for the better in the European attitude towards Islam. But the Europe of the present century is far advanced. It is beginning to be enamoured of the creed of Muhammad. In the next century it may go still further in recognising the utility of that creed in solving its problems and it is in this sense that you must understand my prediction. Already even at the present time many of my own people and of Europe as well have gone over to the faith of Muhammad, and the Islamization of Europe, to use the expression of your own query, may be said to have begun".

That Bernard Shaw is not beside the mark in his forecast regarding the future of Islam, has been proved by an article entitled "Islam's challenge to Christianity," published in the "Catholic Times" of the 18th January 1929. The following note of alarm was sounded in it on behalf of Christianity: "Do we realise that we are faced with a peril which, though as small as a man's hand at present, may assume a formidable shape......This peril is the invasion of Britain by Islam; and those who have eyes to see can have little doubt that it is within our gates. Islam has made enormous strides in Britain ......Muslim converts are found alike amongst the upper, the middle and the lower classes".

John Davenport writes "Is it possible to conceive, we may ask, that the man who effected such great and lasting reforms in his own country by substituting the worship of the one only true God for the gross and debasing idolatry in which his countrymen had been plunged for ages, who

8

abolished infanticide, prohibited the use of spirituous liquors and games of chance (those sources of moral depravity); who restricted within comparatively narrow limits the unrestrained polygamy which he found in existence and practice—can we conceive of so great and zealous a reformer to have been a mere imposter, or that his whole career was one of sheer hypocrisy? Can we imagine that his divine mission was a mere invention of his own of whose falsehood he was conscious throughout? No, surely nothing but a consciousness of really righteous intentions could have carried Muhammad so steadily and constantly without ever flinching or wavering, without ever betraying himself to his most intimate connections and companions, from his first Revelation to Khadija to his last agony in the arms of Ayesha".

"Surely a good and sincere man full of confidence in his Creator, who makes an immense reform both in faith and practice, is truly a direct instrument in the hands of God and may be said to have a commission from Him......"

Cannon Isaac Taylor, who formed a very decided opinion of the civilising power of Islam, writes as follows:—

"It is not the first propagation of Islam that has to be explained, but it is the permanency with which it retains its hold upon its converts. An African tribe, once converted to Islam, never reverts to paganism and never embraces Christianity. When Mohammadanism is embraced by a Negro tribe, paganism, devil-worship, fetishism, cannibalism, human sacrifice, infanticide, witch-craft at once disappear. The natives begin to dress, filth is replaced by cleanliness, drunkenness becomes very rare, gambling is forbidden, the immodest dance and the promiscuous intercourse of the sexes cease. Hospitality becomes a religious duty, female chastity is regarded as a virtue, industry replaces idleness, law, order and sobriety prevail, a feeling of humanity, benevolence and brotherhood is inculcated. Polygamy and slavery are regulated, their evils restrained. Islam, above all, is the most powerful total abstinence association in the world; whereas the extension of European trade means the extension of drunkenness and vice and the degradation of the people. Islam introduces a civilisation of no low order, including a knowledge of reading and writing, decent clothing, personal cleanliness, veracity and self-respect. Its restraining and civilising effects are marvellous. How little have we to show for the vast sums of money and all the precious lives lavished upon Africa? Christian converts are reckoned by thousands, Muslim converts by millions. These are the stern facts we have to face. They are extremely unpleasant facts; it is folly to ignore them. We ought to begin by recognising the fact that Islam is not an anti-Christian faith, but a half Christian faith."

E. E. Kellett in his "A Short History of Religion" says, "In our opinion we may say that Islam was bound to command success as in its teaching about the obedience to God it stands unrivalled in religious scriptures. Even today the old spirit of Father Abraham still actuating the devout Moslem, he considers it his highest duty to do everything that he believes to be the behest of Allah."

"We cannot consider in this place," says Chambers' Encyclopædia, "what Islam has done for the cause of all humanity, or more exactly, what is its share in the development of science and art in Europe. Broadly speaking, the Mohammadans may be said to have been the enlightened teachers of barbarous Europe, from the ninth to the thirteenth century . . . Arabic philosophy, medicine, natural history, geography, history, grammar, rhetoric and the 'golden art of poetry', schooled by the old Hellenic masters, brought forth an abundant harvest of works, many of which will live and teach as long as there will be generations to be taught."

Among non-Muslim sovereigns, Queen Victoria the Good and Napoleon the Great were profoundly impressed by the lofty ideals of Islam. The religion of a people is well reflected in their culture and traditions, and these are best learnt through the language in which they are embodied. Desirous of knowing what Islam, professed by millions of her subjects, really was, Queen Victoria studiously learnt Urdu in her old age. As a language is best learnt by speaking it and hearing it spoken, she sent for a number of Muslim orderlies from India. Through them and her Urdu tutors, Munshi Abdul Karim and Moulvi (now Sir) Rafiuddin Ahmad, she came in close contact with Islam, and realised its great beauties and humanitarian principles. Her estimation of Islam may be gathered from her letters written in 1891 to the wife of the Governor of Bombay, published in the latest volume of her letters. Her Majesty writes, "I think no attempt should be made to interfere with the Muhammadan religion which contains, when known and understood, so much that is fine, to be respected and admired . . . . " The words "when known and understood" are very significant.

Mr. Riply, well-known throughout America, particularly for his "Believe it or not" series of films, who made a careful study of Napoleon's life, definitely stated in the "Express" that he had no doubt that Napoleon while in Egypt had embraced Islam and he lived and died a Muslim, as his frequent reference to this in his conversation not only in France but while a captive at St. Helena, when the cloak of policy and expediency had fallen away from him, clearly proves. In one of his despatches Napoleon wrote, "I hope the time is not far off when I shall be able to establish a uniform regime based upon the principles of the Quran, which alone are true and which alone can lead man to happiness". In an assembly of savants, governors and nobles at Cairo Napoleon declared, "Surely I have told you on different occasions and I have intimated to you by various discourses that I am a unitarian Mussalman and I glorify the prophet Muhammad". That Nepoleon's profession of Islam was not a matter of political expediency, as some people think, has been clearly shown by J. D. Jenkins in the course of a learned article on the "Religious Faith of Napoleon" in which reference has been made to Napoleon's Journal at St. Helena, edited by General Gourgand, who was a devout Roman Catholic.

Among non-Muslim Indian admirers of the prophet of Islam the names of Guru Nanak, Raja Rammohan Roy, Mrs. Sarojini Naidu and Mahatma

In the name of Allah, the most merciful and beneficent.

There is no God but Allah, Muhammad is the Prophet of God.

All praise is due to Allah, the Lord of the universes: He that is all-merciful and beneficent; the Master of the Day of judgment. Thee do we serve and Thee do we beseech for help; guide us on the right path, the path of those on whom Thou hast bestowed favours, not of those on whom Thy wrath has fallen, nor of those who go astray.

O Living, O Permanent, O Pure, O Guardian, O Master, O One, O Depended upon, O All-knowing, O All-informed, O Favourer, O Taha, O Single, O Allah, O Expansive, O Creator, O Originator, O All-merciful, O Beneficent, O Thou Lord of universes.

There is no God but Allah, Muhammad is the Prophet of God. I testify that there is no God but Allah and I testify that Muhammad is His servant and His prophet.

Say that Allah is one; Allah is He on whom all depend; He begets not, nor is He begotton; and there is none like Him.

And God shall be the perfector of His light even though the disbelievers dislike it.

There is no Lord except Thee; praise be to Thee; verily I have been a transgressor.

Verily those who over-reach thee are really over-reaching God: verily God hath full power over all things.

O Living, O Permanent, from Thy benevolence I seek favour.

The God except Him there is no Lord. He is the Living, the Permanent; fatigue seizeth Him not, nor sleep. His is all that there is in the heavens and all there is on earth. Who is the one that can intercede before Him except with His permission. He knoweth all there is between their hands and what is behind them; and they cannot encompass anything of His knowledge except that which He pleaseth. His seat expands over the heavens and the earth, and the safeguarding of them fatigues Him not and He is the All-High and Majestic.

When the help of the Lord comes and there is triumph, and thou seest men entering the religion of God in battalions, then do thou proclaim the praise of thy Lord and crave pardon from Him, for verily He is supremely pardoning.

Verily to God Islam is the religion,
Even though the disbelievers like it not.
Touch it not except those who are purified.
(All the above lines are from verses in the Quran.)

چولہ باوا نانک صاحب

The Robe of Bawa Nanak Saheb.

Gandhi deserve special mention. Nanak, the founder of the Sikh religion, a saint and sage of world-wide reputation, entertained the highest respect and reverence for Islam and its prophet. His passionate love for the Prophet took him all the way to Arabia. He twice performed the pilgrimage to Mecca and visited the Prophet's tomb at Medina. All his teachings breathe an Islamic spirit. The Granth Sahib, the Sikh scripture, is full of references to Islamic doctrines and the Prophet. In one place he writes, "the age for the Vedas and Puranas is gone, now the Quran is the only book to guide the world". The copy of the holy Quran from which the Guru used to read out the divine message, is still to be seen at Guru Hara Sahai in Ferozepur district. Even to this day the famous Chola (garment) which the Guru used to wear has been preserved at Dera Baba Nanak, as a religious relic. As will be seen in the picture, it is profusely imprinted with verses from the Quran. On his death, Nanak's dead body, like that of Kabir, was claimed both by the Hindus and the Muslims.

Had the present-day Sikhs and Muslims been true followers of their respective spiritual heads, they would have never disgraced themselves by fighting each other over trifling matters as they have been doing.

It was but natural that Raja Rammohan Roy, whose profound knowledge of Arabic and Persian earned him the designation of "Zabardust Maulvi," and whose "Tuhfatul-Mowahhydeen" (gift to monotheists) is a vigorous protest against idolatry, should have entertained the highest respect and unstinted admiration for the prophet of Islam.

The following is an extract from an eloquent speech delivered by the talented lady, Mrs. Sarojini Naidu :—

"And if to-day we quote a little from an American writer, and speak of the New World of Islam, it is merely to bring back to the world that has forgotten the message that came to them, that while there is one heart that seeks an ideal, while there is one man that can follow logically to its ultimate issues the ideal of brotherhood, then Islam and the flag of Islam must always reign. What the Western world calls modern, calls new, is nothing but the harvest of that seed that was sown in the oasis of the desert of Arabia. I wonder how many of the Christian ladies to-day realize that the first status of honour, the first status of legal right and responsibility was conferred on woman by the Islamic Faith. How many of my own co-religionists, how many of the Buddhist people, how many of the Christian communities, understand that thirteen hundred years ago a Prophet rose and said: "Chattel! Be thou woman and stand upright and face the sun!"

Mahatma Gandhi, who by his saintly character commands great esteem of the civilised world, wrote on the occasion of one of the birth-day anniversaries of the Prophet: "When the West was sunk in darkness a bright star rose in the firmament and gave light and comfort to a groaning world. In its glorious days, Islam was not intolerant. It commanded the admiration of the world. Let Hindus study it reverently and they will love it as I do . . . . It was not the sword that won a place for Islam in those days in the scheme of life. It was the rigid simplicity, the utter self-effacement of the Prophet, the scrupulous regard for pledges, his intense devotion to his friends and followers, his intrepidity, his fearlessness, his absolute trust in God and in his mission—these, and not the sword, carried everything before them and surmounted every obstacle."

"Some one has said," continues Mahatma Gandhi, "that Europeans in South Africa dread the advent of Islam that civilised Spain, Islam that took the torch-light to Morocco and preached to the world the gospel of brotherhood. The Europeans of South Africa dread the advent of Islam, for they are afraid of the fact that if the native races embrace Islam they may claim equality with the white races. They may well dread it. If brotherhood is a sin, if it is equality of the coloured races that they dread, then that dread is well founded. For, I have seen that any Zulu embracing Christianity does not *ipso-facto* come on a level with the Christians, while immediately he embraces Islam, he drinks from the same cup and eats from the same dish as a Mussalman. That is what they dread."

It will indeed be a happy day for India when the non-Muslims, following the advice of Mahatma Gandhi, will "reverently study Islam and learn to love it," as he does. What can be more regrettable than the fact that Hindus and Muslims, who have to live and die in this the common land of their birth, fly at each other's throat on the flimsiest pretext, often in the name of religion, which is intended to promote peace and good-will among mankind? This shows how far they have strayed away from the high ideals and broad outlook of their respective religions. Is there not much in the faiths and cultures of Hindus and Muslims which both can appreciate, admire and be proud of? There is nothing blameable in furthering the cause of one's own faith by expounding its inherent merits and intrinsic beauties, instead of finding fault with another's faith. This does not engender bitterness of feelings. "For every one of you did we appoint a law and way, and if God had pleased, He would have made you (all) a single community, but that He might try you in what He gave you, therefore, strive with one another to hasten to virtuous deeds." Al-Quran.

The End.

*

APPENDIX

ISLAM'S CONTRIBUTION
TO
SCIENCE & CIVILISATION.

FOREWORD

One of the most potent sources of Hindu-Moslem conflict in India is that we know so little of each other. We live side by side and yet very often our worlds are entirely different. Such mental aloofness has done immense mischief in the past and forebodes an evil future. It is only through a sympathetic understanding of each other's culture and social customs and conventions that we can create an atmosphere of peace and good will. With this end in view I started a few years ago a department of Islamic Culture in Visva Bharati with the generous financial support of His Exalted Highness the Nizam. I am glad to say the experiment has been successful. But work of this sort must be elaborated a hundred fold. Individual educationists and scholars must also take it up and as such I heartily welcome the series of articles from my distinguished countryman, Maulvi Abdul Karim, on Islam's contribution to Science and Civilisation. The writer has clothed his erudition in as simple a garb as possible and the book should have great popular appeal. It is with pleasure that I commend the book to my countrymen.

UTTARAYAN
SANTINIKETAN, BENGAL
August 19, 1935.

(Sd.) RABINDRA NATH TAGORE

*

INTRODUCTION.

History bears incontestable testimony to the fact that Islam gave unprecedented impetus to the intellectual development of the human race and the early Muslims held high the torch of light and learning at a time when the whole world was immersed in ignorance and barbarity. The impression prevalent in Europe that Islam is an unprogressive religion, antagonistic to science and civilisation, is absolutely incorrect. Perhaps no religion has been so greatly misrepresented and misinterpreted by prejudiced and uninformed critics as Islam. Far from adequately appreciating the glorious scientific achievements of the early Muslims and gratefully acknowledging the immense debt the world owes to them, the designing critics have shamelessly calumniated Islam by completely distorting historical facts and wilfully perverting established truths. I hope to prove that it was Islam that gave birth to modern science, inaugurated a scientific era in the world's history and made the early Muslims precursors of modern scientists and pioneers of modern civilisation. The subsequent intellectual stagnation that came upon the Muslim world, giving rise to a false impression regarding Islamic influence, was entirely due to certain historical circumstances similar to those that prevailed in Europe during the Middle Ages, before the Renaissance and the Reformation. The Islamic faith and its teachings were in no way responsible for this social degeneration and political debacle.

CHAPTER I

Islam Furthered the Cause of Science more than any other Religion.

It is now being realised that modern science owes its origin to Islam and modern progress is the outcome of the freedom of thought and spirit of enquiry prescribed for the Muslims by the Holy Quran, and not a product of Christianity, which for a long time relentlessly proscribed all free thinking and liberal reasoning and even scientific researches on original lines, and horribly persecuted all those who indulged in these. The impression that it was Christianity that advanced science and civilisation is, therefore, as erroneous as the idea that Islam hampered their progress. In fact there can be no comparison between Islam and Christianity as civilising forces. While the Muslims rose to the pinnacle of learning in a few centuries after the promulgation of Islam, the Christians remained steeped in ignorance for more than a thousand years.

If Europe's indebtedness to Islam for the extraordinary progress it has latterly made in science and civilisation were adequately known, it would have astounded the modern civilised world. After a careful study of the history of Islam, Canon Isaac Taylor came to the definite conclusion that "Islam has done more for civilisation than Christianity." Arthur Leonard has truly said, "Islam, in fact, has done a work. She has left a mark on the pages of human history, which is so indelible that it can never be effaced . . . . that only when the world grows wiser will be acknowledged in full."

That the early Muslims very largely contributed to the cultural development of the world cannot but be admitted by all unprejudiced and fair-minded critics of Islamic history. It is nothing but religious prejudice and an over-weening sense of racial superiority which have stood in the way of acknowledgment and appreciation by the West of the glorious achievements of the East. Draper is perfectly justified in deploring "the systematic manner in which the literature of Europe has continued to put out of sight our scientific obligations to Mahomedans. Surely they cannot be much longer hidden. Injustice founded on religious rancour and national conceit cannot be perpetrated for ever".

CHAPTER II

Muslims laid the Foundation of Physical Science

It is a historical fact that cannot be controverted that before the advent of Islam, cultivation of science was condemned as heresy. The reason for this is not far to seek. The bulk of mankind could not at that time think in the abstract, and they looked upon the elements of Nature, the subject-matter of science, as sacred objects, possessing supernatural powers. They made idols, symbolizing different elements, and worshipped them as gods and goddesses, either for protection from evil or for attainment of certain objects. Thus were the sun, the moon, the stars, air, water, animals, and even trees and stones, deified and adored. It was nothing unnatural in such circumstances that any deviation from the prevailing belief in their sanctity should have been branded as a sacrilege, and any attempt at a critical examination of their potentiality, for good or evil, stigmatised as profanity. Thus all that was useful in the heavens and the earth remained altogether unexplored, and for thousands of years man did not realise the sublime utility of the forces of Nature. It was reserved for the untutored Son of the Desert to open man's eyes to the wonderland of Nature by bringing down her elements from the high pedestal of divinity, on which they had been placed, to the position of servants of mankind.

The Subservience of Natural Elements to Man

"And He has made subservient to you the night and the day and the sun and moon and the stars are made subservient by His commandment ; most surely there are signs in this for a people to ponder . . . . " Al-Quran.

Thus were the gods of the pre-Islamic people reduced by one stroke to man's servants. For the first time in the history of the world the Holy Quran declared in unmistakable language that the main purpose for which all objects, from the mightiest sun to the most insignificant atom, were created, is to minister to man's needs. Everything in the universe being intended for his use, man has been commanded to investigate their intrinsic properties,—in other words, to cultivate every branch of science. Thus did the Quran, by declaring man the lord of the universe and everything in it subservient to him, give a tremendous impetus to the development of scientific research. In fact the foundation of modern science was thus laid by acquainting man with the real nature of the forces and laws of Nature and by teaching him how to harness them for human service. The initiation of the conquest of Nature and the utilisation of its forces for the good of humanity is, indeed, one of the greatest blessings Islam has conferred upon mankind.

The Quran clearly indicated the way in which to reduce Nature to human service by contemplation and observation of four kinds, viz., *Tafaqquh, Tadabbur, Tafakkur* and *Taaqqul*. By the first a correct idea of things and their different features can be got, by the second the knowledge of how to utilise them properly can be acquired, the third teaches the ways by which things have come into existence and how their properties may be discovered, while the fourth gives the knowledge which enables man to make the right use of different things in every-day life. It was the meditations indicated by *Tafakkur* and *Taaqqul* that actuated different kinds of scientific research among the early Muslims. This is how the Quran placed in the hands of man the key with which the treasure-house of Nature could be opened, and Divine Revelation came to show him the way to his material progress. Everything in the universe having been intended for the use of man, it was a virtuous act for him to make researches into the realms of Nature in order to discover the utility of its various components. Thus the first principle of progress, the utilisation of the forces of Nature for the needs of man, became an article of faith with the Muslims, and impelled them to engage in scientific research.

Nature's Exploration is God's Glorification

The Prophet of Islam went so far as to make explorations in the realms of Nature the real glorification of God, and to place the acquisition of knowledge on an equal footing with His worship. Man was required to glorify God not by mere expression of lip-gratitude, but by discovering and utilising the properties and potentialities of the things He has created for supplying the needs of His creatures. Realisation of the scattered bounties of God was to be the realisation of God Himself. A Muslim was to spiritualise, as it were, his whole material surroundings by seeing and feeling the evidence of God's power and love in every blade of grass and in every breath of air.

"Verily in the creation of heavens and earth, and the alteration of night and day, there are signs for men of understanding, who remember Allah standing, sitting and while lying on their sides, and ponder over the creation of heavens and earth" (and say) "our Lord Thou hast not created (all) this in vain. Glory be to Thee". Al-Quran.

Islam made Reason the Test of Faith

Before the advent of Islam learning was confined to the chosen few. The masses had to accept blindly whatever was placed before them as their religion and they were not permitted to use their intellect or judgment. In fact, before the promulgation of Islam religion was synonymous with dogmas and doctrines, rites and rituals ; and bigotry had placed an embargo on freedom of thought and enquiry. Whenever any one conceived any new idea or propounded a new theory, he was condemned by his co-religionists as a heretic. Some of the most inhuman atrocities ever committed on men in search of truth were thus perpetrated in the name of religion. It was Islam that for the first time discountenanced all dogmatic teachings and made reason the test of faith. "The first thing created," says the Prophet of Islam, "was reason. God has not created anything better than reason". On another occasion the Propdet said, "Verily a man has performed prayers, fasts, charity and pilgrimages and all other good deeds, but he will not be rewarded save in proportion to the sense he employs". According to the Quran "There is no piety in turning your face towards the East or the West". *Iman* (faith) means knowledge of a truth or principle with such a conviction as to its truth as will incite one to live up to it. It does not signify belief that cannot be translated into action. All this unmistakably demonstrates that Islam does not regard rituals and ceremonies as essentials of religion. In fact, mere dogmatic doctrines have no significance for a true Muslim, who has to observe his religion in every deed and action, in every thought and conception. He may indulge in free thought and free enquiry concerning everything that man's intelligence is capable of apprehending. To him science, the aim of which is truth, is the greatest ally of true religion. "Islam stands almost alone," says Guizot in his History of European Civilisation, "among the religions in discountenancing the reliance on tradition without argument. It demands that its votaries should undertake the investigation of the great work of their faith". Miracle has no place in Islam to which Nature itself is a revelation of God, and its laws His eternal miracles, demonstrating His Majesty, His Omnipotence and His Benevolence. In fact man knew nothing of God except through His work in Nature. Islam thus gave to scientific research a religious aspect unknown and unthought of before.

By thus putting an end to all conflicts between religion and science and by making the first principle of scientific progress—the subservience of Nature to man—an article of faith, Islam revolutionised the human mind, imparted immense energy and initiative to it and greatly impelled it to investigate the marvels of creation. Moreover, it immeasurably enlarged the scope of religion, which had till then been regarded only as a means of man's future salvation, but now, for the first time, came to be looked upon also as an effective factor in his material advancement. Every branch of learning conducive to human well-being and progress thus came within the purview of Islam, which harmonised the esoteric and exoteric sides of man's life. Thus modern progress had its origin in the spirit of free thought and investigation engendered by Islam.

Islam made Education Compulsory for all

I have already stated what Islam did for two of the most important factors of modern culture and civilisation. Let us now see what it did for another important factor, *viz.*, dissemination of knowledge. It is a historical fact that no messenger of God, from Noah to Jesus, had done anything worth mentioning for the dissemination of knowledge, which was selfishly monopolised by a few priests and theologians, anxious to retain all power in their own hands. But the Prophet of Islam, though he himself knew not how to read and write, laid the greatest stress on the acquisition of knowledge and made it essentially incumbent upon all his followers, irrespective of sex and rank ; *Talabul-Ilme Farizatun Ala Kulle Muslimin Wa Muslimatin :* "Seeking of knowledge is imperative for all Muslims, male and female". "He who has been gifted with knowledge", says the Quran, "has been gifted with an abounding blessing". Convinced that an ignorant person cannot adequately realise the greatness and goodness of God, the Prophet of Islam made acquisition of knowledge an essential of faith and did not approve of his followers being entirely absorbed in the meditation of God, "an hour's contemplation and study of His creation being better than a year's adoration". Muslims were particularly enjoined to be in constant search of knowledge "from the cradle to the grave," and they were told that "the ink of the scholar was holier than the blood of the martyr".

Thus in that dark age, when the world was enveloped in ignorance and illiteracy, Islam created an insatiable thirst for knowledge and caused a tremendous upheaval of science in realms hitherto altogether unexplored. Such an extraordinary outburst of intellectual activity was unparalleled in human history. Some undreamt of discoveries and inventions were made and these immensely contributed to the progress of civilisation and the welfare of mankind. There was hardly any science of which the Muslims did not make themselves masters. They created modern Chemistry, made most important discoveries in Astronomy, added much to the knowledge of Mathematics and Medicine and made very valuable researches in Botany, Geology and other branches of Natural Philosophy. The foundation of what is termed Physical Science was thus laid, and the gates of investigation into the marvels of creation were flung wide open.

The Muslims, by unravelling the mysteries of Nature and widening the scope of knowledge, introduced such blessings of comfort and happiness as were unknown in the world. It was the intellectual liberty and the spirit of scientific research inaugurated by them that brought about the European Renaissance and introduced into the modern world the arts and sciences which ennobled the heart, elevated the mind and contributed to human happiness.

The height of scientific progress forecast by the Quran has not yet been fully attained. The world is full of materials that await man's exertion and ingenuity for their development and utilisation. There are millions of things in the realm of the seas and in the bowels of the earth and the ocean that have been created for man's use. All these have to be harnessed in order to meet the increased requirements of human society. The Quran repeatedly speaks of the subservience of the physical world and phenomena to man, whose duty it is to explore them for use.

Before the advent of Islam, the West, which now-a-days claims all credit for progress in science and civilisation, was steeped in ignorance and darkness. It was the intellectual liberty and scientific research inaugurated by the Muslims which brought about the Renaissance to which Europe owed its regeneration. Medieval Europe was a hot-bed of religious fanaticism and social conservatism ; and the intellectual stagnation which prevailed there is altogether beyond conception in modern times.

Persecution of Scientists in the West

In medieval Europe religion and science were thought to be quite irreconcilable to each other, and whoever ventured to express any opinion contrary to the prevailing sacerdotal belief was not merely branded as a heretic, but was relentlessly persecuted, inhumanly tortured and even mercilessly put to death. For his belief in the theory of evolution, Vanini's tongue was torn out of his mouth and he was burnt alive. Hypatia, the renowned commentator on Plato, had to pay the penalty for her intellectual audacity with her life. Copernicus tried to demonstrate that the earth revolves and not the heavens. Thereupon even Martin Luther denounced him as "an upstart astrologer," and Calvin most severely condemned him. He had, therefore, to end his life in disgrace. Bruno, who dared to advance the Copernican theory, was seized, imprisoned and at last put to death by a "fire made slow to increase the torture". Galileo, who supported the Copernican theory, was thrown into a dungeon, horribly tortured and forced to recant as follows :—"I, Galileo, being in my seventieth year, being a prisoner on my knees before your Eminences having before my eyes the Holy Gospel, abjure, curse and detest the error and the heresy of the movements of the Earth". Not content with mere recantation, the Holy Inquisition sent him into exile for the rest of his life. Thus many a devoted votary of science fell a victim to Christian fanaticism prevalent in the Middle Ages, and some famous libraries, containing the accumulated treasure of age, were consigned to the flames.*

* The allegation that Muslims destroyed the Alexandria Library is not true. This Library was founded during the time of the first Ptolemy Demtrius Phabreus. It had then a collection of 50,000 volumes, and in the course of time the number of books reached 7,00,000. It contained the valuable literature of Rome, Greece, Egypt and India. When Julius Cæsar beseiged Alexandria, the major portion of the library was set on fire and the literary wealth of ages, hoarded by those aspiring after knowledge, was reduced to ashes. It was, however, once again replaced by the collection of Pergamos and presented to Cleopatra by Mark Antony. The remaining portion of the library which was shifted to the famous temple of Serapeum was destroyed by a fanatical mob of Christians led on by Archbishop Theophilus, acting on the decree of the Christian King Theodorus, according to which all the heathen temples in Rome together with the valuable literary treasures were destroyed in 391 A.D.

All this conclusively proves that the credit given to Christianity, as a religion, for promoting the cause of science, is nothing but a travesty of truth.

CHAPTER III.

Western Civilisation is the direct offspring of Arab Civilisation in Spain

It is an uncontroverted truth that modern progress in the West was not the outcome of Man's faith In Church dogmas. In fact the West made no progress worth the name as long as it was in the iron grip of Christianity. This is borne out by the fact that centuries of domination of Spain, France, England and other countries of Europe by the Romans, who had embraced Christianity, could not remove from them the utter darkness in which they were groping and the appalling ignorance in which they were immersed. The extraordinary progress made by the Christian countries during the last five hundred years is directly due to the teachings of Islam, which was promulgated six hundred years after Christianity. It was not till freedom of thought was

---

A Christian writer invented a story that the Alexandria Library was destroyed by the Muslims at the time of Khalifa Omar after the conquest of Alexandria in 641 A.D. There is strong evidence to show that no library existed at Alexandria at that time. Besides, a great patron of learning as Omar was, such an act of vandalism was totally against his liberal and tolerant spirit and quite incompatible with the religion he professed.

advocated and the torch of learning was lighted by the Muslims in Spain that any progress in science and civilisation could be made in Europe, or any possibility could arise for the Renaissance and the Reformation to make their appearance in the Christian world. It was from Muslim Spain that a new life dawned upon the whole of Europe, giving birth to a new culture which greatly stimulated the intellectual activity of its people. All that Christian Europe learnt of Greek and Hindu Philosophy and Science up to the Renaissance period emanated from the Saracenic culture of Spain.

After the conquest of Spain the Muslims established there several Universities which opened their doors to all students without distinction of creed, caste, colour or country ; and also boarded and lodged them at public expense. Spain thus became the centre of European culture and scholars from all parts of Christian Europe flocked to her seats of learning. Rogers, Bacon and other pioneers of the Rationalist movement in Europe, all received their education in the Muslim University of Cordova. Even the great Emperor Charlemagne had to send his son to Spain to be educated by the Muslim teachers, for nowhere else in Europe was there any seat of learning worthy of the name.

Every branch of science was seriously investigated in Muslim Spain. Medicine received greater development by the discoveries of her doctors and surgeons than it had gained during all the centuries that had elapsed since the days of Galen. Astronomy, Chemistry, Geography, Natural History, all were studied at Cordova with great ardour ; as for the graces of literature, there never was such a time when poetry became almost the common speech of every body. "The taste for science and literature," writes Renan, "had by the tenth century established, in this privileged corner of the world, a toleration of which modern times hardly offer us an example. Christians, Jews and Muslims spoke the same tongue, sang the same songs, and participated in the same literary and scientific studies". All the barriers which separated the various peoples were effaced ; all strove with one accord in the work of a common civilisation. The mosques of Cordova, where the students could be counted by the thousands, became the active centres of philosophical and scientific studies. "It must be owned," observes John Davenport, "that all the knowledge whether of physics, astronomy, philosophy or mathematics, which flourished in Europe from the tenth century, was originally derived from the Arabian schools, and the Spanish Saracen may be looked upon as the father of European philosophy".

Some idea of the architectural beauty and grandeur introduced into Europe by the Muslims may be had from the Alhambra Court in the Crystal Palace in London. Stanley Lane-Pool in "The Moors in Spain" has well described all this ; he says, "Beautiful as were the palaces and gardens of Cordova, her claims to admiration in higher matters were no less strong. The mind was as lovely as the body".

As rightly acknowledged by Gustav Diercks in his "Europe's Debt to Islam," there can be no denying that Europe is deeply in debt to Islam for all its scientific discoveries. In fact it was Islam that produced scientists who anticipated Bacon, Newton, Kepler and other great scientists of Europe. But for the introduction into Europe by the Muslims of paper, gunpowder, the mariner's compass and such other instruments of progress, who knows that the condition of Europe in respect of science and civilisation would not have been to-day what it was fourteen hundred years ago.

The industries developed by the Muslims during their rule in Spain were many and of far-reaching consequence. Ship-building, horticulture, vanyards, glassware, silver mines, cotton manufactures, silks, woolen carpets, iron and copper utensils and inlaid metal work were some of these. The Muslims gave Europe the mulberry tree, the maize, the sugar-cane, the wind-mill and many such other items of industry. During the reign of the Spanish king, Al-Hakam, great irrigation systems were developed in Granada, Valencia and Arragon. In short, the art of war, industry, commerce and seamanship made unprecedented progress in Muslim Spain. It is a historical fact that 477 years before Columbus, the Arabs and the Moors of Spain traded with the American continent.

Though the average Westerner is under the impression that Europe's salvation was caused by the defeat of the Muslims at Tours (Poitiers), the real fact is that the world's progress was retarded for ages by this check on the advance of the Muslims in the West. Perhaps the darkest pages in the annals of history, dealing with the Inquisition and such other disgraceful matters, would never have been written at all and the Renaissance, which ushered in an era of civilisation in Europe, would have been accelerated by seven hundred years if the Muslims had won that battle and Islamised the whole of Europe. Anatole France, who was above racial and religious prejudice, truly said in his *La Vie En Flour,* "The most tragic event in history is that of the Battle of Poitiers, when the science, the art and the civilisation of Arabia fell before the barbarism of the Franks".

It is indeed a most happy sign of the times that not only fair-minded individuals, whose illuminating observations have been quoted, but even a whole nation has at last realised that Europe's extraordinary progress in science and civilisation, which has given her a dominating position all the world over, is to be ascribed to the civilising force of Islam. As a mark of belated justice, the Spanish Republic is arranging to establish an Arabic University in Madrid in order to commemorate what Islam achieved for science and civilisation during the Muslim occupation of Spain. It is hoped this will enlighten the world about the fact that the Muslims were the most zealous promoters and protectors of knowledge and culture for full one thousand years, during which other peoples were enshrouded in ignorance, bigotry and barbarism.

CHAPTER IV

Intellectual Achievements of early Muslims

It is now an undisputed fact that the early Muslims made incomparable contributions to the culture and civilisation of the world. Far from proscribing free thought and enquiry and placing any ban upon the cultivation of science, as early and medieval Christianity did, Islam gave it a tremendous impetus by making it a part of religion itself. A Muslim was enjoined to look upon the universe as an expression of God's attributes, and he had to explore it and utilise its objects for the service of mankind as an item of worship of their Creator. It was this religious stimulus to scientific research that particularly impelled the early Muslims so zealously to exert themselves for the advancement of science. A detailed account of their numerous scientific achievements would fill many volumes. The more the world advances in civilisation the more will their inestimable services to humanity be adequately realised and appreciated.

History bears witness to the fact that it was Islam that raised some of the most backward nations to the highest pinnacle of moral and material progress. Wherever the Muslims conquered a country, instead of slaughtering the vanquished, as was done by the Israelites of old, they gave them new life, inspired them with lofty ideals and raised them to a high level of civilisation. Thus, indeed, were many savage tribes transformed into civilised people. To whatever land the Arabs migrated they made it their home ; they absorbed the culture of the conquered people and they did their best for the intellectual, moral and material improvement of the land of their adoption. The people to whom the later intellectual development of the Muslims was due were, for the most part, not Arabs, but descendants of those who had adopted the faith of the conquerors. Wherever the banner of Islam was carried, remarkable centres of learning sprang up in no time, and produced illustrious men in the fields of literature, arts, science and industry. Thus, Damascus, Cordova, Granada, Baghdad, and Cairo became, from time to time, reputed centres of Muslim culture, and held aloft the torch of light and learning, art and science in Asia, Europe and Africa, at a time when the West was sunk in ignorance and superstition.

Europe's indebtedness to Islam for her scientific progress is much greater than she cares to admit. She remained barren of all progress as long as she was under the heel of the Church. Even the intellectual development that had taken place among the Greeks and the Romans disappeared under the persecution of the Church. During the centuries of moral and intellectual stagnation in Europe, it was the Muslims who led the vanguard of intellectual progress in the world. There was a time when learning in Europe could be obtained only through the medium of the Arabic tongue. The very Renaissance, that awakened her from her long lethargy, was brought about by the impact of Islamic culture and learning. But for the conquest of Spain by the Muslims, who knows how long she would have remained in that savage condition. All her later achievements in the domain of science, art and learning owe their inspiration wholly and solely to the influences that emanated from Muslim Spain and penetrated the rest of the continent. All knowledge, whether of Astronomy, Mathematics, Physics or Philosophy, of which later on the Europeans made themselves masters, was originally derived from the Saracenic schools. Besides, there has been hardly any reform, religious, social or political, from the time of Martin Luther to that of Lenin, which does not bear the stamp of Islamic influence. Draper has very truly said, "In whatever direction we look we meet in various pursuits of peace and war, of letter and science, Saracenic vestiges".

Dr. Campbell, a reputed British scientist, in his book, "Arabian Medicine", writes, "When Europe was lying torpid in the depth of intellectual obscurity and gloom in the dark ages, culture and civilisation were spread in the Islamic States under the high patronage of the Caliphs of Baghdad and Cordova, and at a time when the Barons and Ladies of Medieval Europe could not even sign their names, almost every adolescent boy and girl in Islam could read and write freely and with ease".

In his famous "History of Human Society," Professor Frank Blackmore of the University of Kansas writes, "In every country that was conquered, the first duty of Islam was to build a mosque in which Allah would be worshipped and his Prophet honoured. Attached to this mosque was a school where people were taught to read and study the Koran. From this initial point they enlarged the study of science, literature and art, and, through the appreciation of these sublime things, they collected the treasures of art and learning wherever these could be found. From imitation they passed on to the great field of creation, and great advances were made to the sum of human knowledge. Schools were founded, great universities established, and libraries were built which laid the permanent foundations of knowledge".

The Muslims made phenomenal progress in Science in a wonderfully short time. They visualised, thirteen centuries ago, many things which are being discovered to-day. They explored and exploited the potentialities of objects which were unknown and unthought-of since the creation of the world. In fact there was hardly any conceivable subject to which they did not give serious thought. They made most important discoveries in Chemistry, in Astronomy, in Mathematics, in Medicine. They unearthed Alchemy and Algebra. They initiated and developed the study of Political Economy and Sociology which were unknown sciences till then. They made valuable researches in Zoology, Geology and Botany. Muslim students, accompanied by artists, travelled far and wide to study various vegetations, which were minutely described by pen and brush. Alherin, a renowned botanist, travelled to and fro in India for forty years collecting materials for his studies. Besides, Muslims investigated and wrote on various other subjects such as navigation, agriculture, irrigation, gardening, statistics, chronology and topography. Even aviation, the latest achievement of Europe and an early wonder of the twentieth century, was not left untried.

The first two martyrs among the conquerors of the air were Muslims. In the reign of Khalifa Al-Mamun, a scientist named Abul Quasim invented an aeroplane, but crashed when flying and was killed.

In the eighth century, the Abbaside Khalifas established the famous academy of Baghdad, where were translated the works of the renowned mathematicians Euclid, Archemedes and Appollonius, of the astronomer Ptolemy, and of the naturalists, Hippocrates and Diomedes. In this and other Muslim centres of learning Greek culture was kept alive at a time when, outside Byzantium, it had no abiding place in the non-Muslim world. Many were the libraries, observatories and laboratories that were established by Muslim kings. In the library attached to Baitul-ul-Hikmat, the abode of learning, a remarkable university founded by Khalifa Harun-ur-Rashid, there were hundreds of thousands of Sanskrit, Greek, Coptic, Chaldean, and Persian books, besides those in Arabic. Khalifa Al-Hakim's library was so very extensive that its catalogue had to be prepared in forty large volumes.

Chemistry.—Modern Chemistry, as Humboldt rightly says, was "admittedly the invention of the Muslims," whose achievements in this sphere were of unique interest. They conclusively proved the worthlessness of ancient chemistry. They found out the chemical affinities of mercury, lead, copper, silver and gold and knew the chemical processes of oxidation and clacination. A number of words, such as alembic, alkali, etc., were derived from Arabic. Jabir-bin-Hayyan, known as Geber in the Western world, wrote some five hundred treatises on chemistry. He discovered, for the first time, nitric acid, sulphuric acid, aqua regia, silver nitrate and several other compounds. The Muslims were the first to teach the world distillation, filtration, crystallisation etc. They knew how to change a liquid into vapour. It was in Muslim Spain that Chemistry was first established in Europe, and would have reached its zenith there had the Muslims not suffered the disastrous defeat at Poitiers. Jildaki was the last great Muslim chemist. He died in 1361 A. D.

Astronomy.—The Muslims may be said to have stamped their name on heaven itself. They indentified and classified a large number of stars in their observatories. They made wonderful discoveries concerning the movements of the solar system and other astral bodies. They ascertained the size of the earth, the variation of the lunar latitudes and the precession of the equinoxes. Averroes (Ibn-i-Rushd) discovered the sun-spot : Al-Hazan (Abul Hasan) discovered atmospheric reflection ; Al-Maimun determined the obliquity of the ecliptic ; Ibn-i-Junus, Nasiruddin Tusi and Al-bani constructed astronomical tables of great value. Albani's tables were translated into Latin and formed the basis of astronomical study in Europe, whither that science was introduced by the translation of the works of Muhammad Farghani. Abu Junus and Al-Batan were two of the greatest Muslim astronomers. It was the Muslims who first built observatories in Europe and invented the telescope, the compass, the pendulum and many other useful astronomical instruments. The most famous of the many observatories in the Muslim Empire was that at Marghana near Taurus, built in 1259 A. D.

Mathematics.—Almost every branch of higher mathematics bears the impress of Muslim genius. Many were the improvements that were effected by the Muslims in this important subject. The Arabic numerals, the decimal system and the art of figures, which Europe got from the Muslims, gave great impetus to learning. By means of these the Muslims led the world in Astronomy, Mechanics and Mathematics. Algebra, Statics, Conic Sections and other branches of applied Mathematics are amongst Muslim discoveries. In Geometry the Muslims were the first of all nations to translate Euclid and use it. It was not properly translated in any European language till the sixteenth century. The Muslims for the first time applied Algebra to Geometry. They discovered equations of the second degree, and developed the theory of quadratic equations and the binomial theorem. They invented spherical Trigonometry and by introducing the use of Sine and Cosine, they made great contributions to the science of surveying and astronomy. The Muslims were the first to use instruments of precision for the measurement of time by the use of the pendulum and the measurement of heavenly bodies by the use of the astrolabe.

Medicine.—The father of the present-day European medical science was Avicenna (Abu-Sina), whose Materia Medica is still in vogue. Aven Zoor (Ibn-i-Zoar) was a great authority on pharmacy, which was an institution of Muslim invention. He and others carefully studied the effect on the body of drugs obtained from various parts of the world, and discovered many remedies. The Muslim doctors were the first to use anæsthetics. Al-Bucasis of Cordova was an expert surgeon of world-wide reputation. There were renowned surgeons, opticians, dentists and specialists in female diseases. The science of optics owes much to Muslim research. Al-Hazan, who understood the weight of air, corrected the misconceptions of the Greeks as to the nature of vision and demonstrated, for the first time in history, that the rays of light come from the external object to the eye, and not from the eye itself impinging on external things. He showed that the retina is the seat of vision, and proved that impressions made upon it were conveyed along the nerves to the brain. He discovered that the refraction of light varied with the density of the atmosphere, and *vice versa*.

In Baghdad, there were no less than 860 doctors of different classes, each class of whom made one particular branch of medicine their special study. Doctors as well as chemists had to pass an examination in order to obtain a license to practise. There were hospitals throughout the wide Muslim empire. All classes of people, irrespective of their creed, caste, colour and country, were freely admitted to these hospitals.

Geography & History.—There are in Arabic many immortal works on Geography. The spherical shape of the globe was demonstrated by the Muslims at a time when the scientists of priest-ridden Europe emphatically asserted that it was flat. The great historical achievements of the Muslims are too well-known to require detailed mention. They produced several thousand books on history, ranging in magnitude from one to eighty volumes.

To sum up, for about one thousand years the Muslims made history ; they held aloft the torch of light and learning and spread knowledge and culture throughout the world. But for the vast intellectual heritage bequeathed by them to the people of the West, it would not have been possible to make the immense progress they have now made. The Muslims were in the vanguard of the world's advancement as long as they were true to Islam and faithfully followed the lofty injunctions of the Holy Quran. Their downfall commenced as soon as they became remiss in their loyalty to the lofty ideals of Islam. With the Western people the reverse has happened. They were not able to make any progress worth the name as long as they were orthodox Christians ; it was only after they had shaken off the grip of Christianity that they could make any appreciable advance in science and civilisation. In the one case the influence of a peaceful and progressive religion and in the other the effect of the disappearance of religious fervour and the presence of materialistic greed are clearly observable in the history of their respective notable achievements. The pre-Islamic religions confined their operation to the moral aspect of human nature, and almost altogether ignored its worldly aspect. But Islam, in addition to morality, laid much stress on the practical aspect of man's every-day life. Under the inspiration of Islam, the chief mission of which is the service of humanity, the Muslims attended to such useful subjects as were calculated to contribute to the material welfare of mankind. Realising that man's material progress depends upon his mastery over nature, they devoted themselves to the development of useful sciences, such as chemistry, astronomy, medicine, agriculture, irrigation, navigation, etc. Had the idea of man's capabilities to harness the forces of Nature to the service of humanity dawned on the human mind before the Holy Prophet of Islam taught it, the immense potentialities of Nature would have been utilised for the welfare of mankind long before the promulgation of Islam.

Most of the outstanding achievements of the people over whom religion has little influence and who are guided more by the fear of man than by the fear of God, have been in the domain of arms, ammunition, explosives, poisons—of death and destruction rather than of peace and construction. Had their religion had sufficient influence over them, the followers of Christ, who enjoins the turning of one cheek if the other is smitten, would have never been so very eager for the invention of all sorts of death-dealing instruments.

After the enjoyment of power, wealth and supremacy for about a thousand years, the Muslims became enervated and luxurious, and a sort of blight overtook them. Spiritual stagnation and intellectual sterility soon followed as a natural consequence. This has more or less been the case with all other religious communities. The Muslims themselves, and not Islam, are entirely to blame for this regrettable check on their progress. A glance at the conditions of the world before and after the promulgation of Islam would convince one of what it is capable of accomplishing. The decadence of the Muslims must not, therefore, be confused with that of their religion. It would be a great injustice to Islam to judge it by the life led by its present-day followers. True Islam, which is life and light, is very different from what goes by its name to-day—a bundle of dead rites and meaningless rituals.

It is, however, gratifying to note that Muslims are at last realising that they have left the essentials of their noble religion and are now engaged in controversies over mere trifles. I believe true Islam will again assert itself. Signs of Islamic renaissance are already visible all over the Muslim world. Movements pregnant with great potentialities are afoot in Turkey, Persia, Arabia, Egypt and Afghanistan. It is hoped that, before long, Muslims would shake off the langour and lethargy that have come upon them, and they will be able to take their rightful place in the progressive movements of the world.

---

*

*

PROPHET OF ISLAM AND HIS TEACHINGS

OPINIONS

It is refreshing in the midst of the sectarian wrangles with which the Muslims are generally occupied, to come across a noble attempt, such as the one made by Maulavi Abdul Karim Sahib . . . . Books of this type are the greatest need of the day, as by clearing misunderstandings about Islam they do a useful service to the cause of humanity.

(MAULANA) MUHAMMAD ALI
(Renowned translator of the Quran)

I was on my sick-bed when I read the "Prophet of Islam". It was refreshing as the breeze of heaven and I read the book without a stop. I could not wish for a better tonic. I congratulate the author on his beautiful presentation of Islam—simple, sincere and devout. . . .

(SIR) B. L. MITTER (K.C.S.I.)

The clear and straight-forward presentation of the essentials of Islam, freed from non-essentials which really provoke unnecessary and harmful controversy, is admirably suited to give Muslims a correct idea of Islam and of its universal nature while creating a sympathetic understanding of our faith among non-Muslims. Such publications are bound to advance the cause of unity in India. The book should be in the hand of every young man in the country irrespective of the community to which he belongs.

AHMED HUSSAIN
(Nawab Aminjung)

This is a very opportune publication. The teachings of the Prophet are often misconstrued and misapplied. A correct understanding of them will go a good way towards removal of misunderstandings and communalism. May the author's noble efforts bear fruits.

(SIR) P. C. ROY

I have read the "Prophet of Islam" with great interest and consider it a welcome addition to the growing literature about the life and work of our great Prophet. . . . .

(SIR) ABDUL QADIR
(Member, Council of Secretary of State)

I think the book should be read by men and women of all creeds and nationalities, so that they may realise that, "As many faiths so many paths". . . . The book is a symbol of internationalism and universal brotherhood of man.

(MAHARAJA SIR) MANMATHA NATH
ROY CHAUDHURY of Santosh

I have read the book with great interest. As the modern educated man knows so little of the past services rendered by Islam, the book should prove to be of considerable utility.

(SIR) S. M. SULAIMAN
(Chief Justice, Allahabad High Court)

. . . . The two sister communities which are destined to live side by side in India and can never think of severing from each other however much their differences may be, do in fact know very little of each other. A mutual understanding is really all that is necessary to cement them together, and for this end this book will be of priceless value.

(SIR) MANMATHA NATH MUKHERJEE
(Judge, Calcutta High Court)

The book, which is an erudite exposition of the spirit of Islam, will have, I hope, a very wide circulation, especially among non-Muslims in India whose profound ignorance of the life of the Prophet and the true spirit of Islam, is largely responsible for communal troubles. It would be an excellent thing if it could be prescribed as a text-book in all high English schools in India. I hope it will be translated into all the important vernaculars in India before long.

GHAZANFER ALI KHAN (I.C..S)
(Retired Divisional Commissioner, C. P.)

I have read the "Prophet of Islam" with not only great interest but great profit as well. Apart from the author's mastery of the English language, the book is a testimony to his enthusiasm for research. . . . The book,

I am sure, will command universal praise and admiration and will lead to a better understanding of the Muslim faith.

(RAI BAHADUR) P. C. DUTT (C.I.E.).
(Member, Executive Council, Assam)

It is a thought-provoking publication and will, I am sure, prove useful not only to Muslims but also to non-Muslims.

I greatly appreciate the author's Islamic sentiments and the solid work he has been doing. I hope and pray he will live long to do the constructive work he has taken in hand and to be one of the very few Muslims, who feel for their community and country.

(NAWAB SIR) ABDUL QAIUM.
(Minister of Education, Frontier Province)

The Prophet of Islam, which is the latest manifestation of Maulvi Abdul Karim's Islamic fervour, is a life story of the Holy Prophet in sweet simple English. . . . Being the outcome of a devout soul, the book makes a direct appeal to the heart of the reader . . . May Maulvi Abdul Karim be spared long to carry on the noble work of enlightening the world as to the true message of Islam, a work to which there is such a widespread indifference among the Muslims.

THE LIGHT, Lahore.

Maulvi Abdul Karim has seen much of the world in different capacities and has used his experience and erudition in the preparation of this work that would bring

not only the hostile critics of Muhammad to a recognition of the truths about the Prophet of Islam and his message but also present before the Muslims themselves an account of Muhammad's life from the cradle to the grave that would make them love and revere their Prophet all the more.

After throwing a flood of light from different angles on the life of the great Arabian Prophet the learned author gives a convincing discourse on the various phases of Islam and its Holy Book while in an appendix he points out Europe's indebtedness to Islam for her scientific and intellectual achievements. We warmly welcome Maulvi Sahib's book, commend it to our readers and wish it a success worthy of its author and its contents.

THE ADVANCE, Calcutta.

Within the narrow compass of this small book Maulvi Abdul Karim has presented to us in his usual simple style the essentials of the life of the Prophet and his teachings. A perusal of this book clearly reveals that Islam is not antagonistic to any religion . . . In these days of religious fanaticism and communal bitterness the publication of this book will do immense good to our countrymen. It should be read by Moslems and non-Moslems alike. It will make the former realise the true ideal of Islam and remove the false prejudices against this great religion from the latter.

AMRITA BAZAR PATRIKA, Calcutta.

We welcome the "Prophet of Islam" from the pen of Maulvi Abdul Karim, a writer of broad outlook, catholic thought, and a student of comparative religious literature . . . . He has done a great service to Hindu-Muslim amity by writing his valuable books, which should be especially read by non-Muslims.

THE HINDUSTAN REVIEW, Patna.

Maulvi Abdul Karim is a Muslim divine of deep learning and catholic sympathies. His "Prophet of Islam" is an excellent brochure, which succinctly sums up the pristine purity of the essentials of Islam . . . . It is a remarkably well-written book and will be profitably read by Muslims and non-Muslims alike.

THE TRIBUNE, Lahore.

This is one of the best books on the subject we have read. The learned author presents the life of Muhammad and his teachings in the most favourable light that is possible . . . . Non-Muslims cannot have a better guide to study the life of Muhammad and his high ideals.

FEDERATED INDIA, Madras.

The author is a person of great learning. The book in brief words explains all the essentials of Islam which looks quite different from what it is believed to be now-a-days. . . . . The book is excellently written and we commend it to our Muslim and non-Muslim readers who must all profit by its study.

THE KASHMIR TIMES.

The book is not voluminous : its brevity is its virtue. . . . It should be placed in the hands of our young men, Hindus and Muslims, to enable the first to understand the religion of Islam and to disarm mental hostility, and the second to realise the beauties of their religion and particularly its underlying spirit of toleration, one of the most beautiful points of their great faith.

THE UNITED INDIA AND INDIAN STATES.

Many, especially many non-Muslims, who have meagre knowledge of Islam and its great prophet, will find in this comparatively small work most of the things one ought to know about them. . . . The Muslims will also find the work highly useful in as much as it imparts in a nutshell, a definite and correct idea of what Islam is, what it stands for and what service it and its Prophet have rendered to humanity at large. . . . . We have much pleasure in commending the book to every English-knowing man and woman.

THE MUSSALMAN, Calcutta.

To the Indian Muslims Maulvi Abdul Karim Sahib is well-known as an educationist and he is considered an able exponent of Islam. . . . The "Prophet of Islam" concludes with a fervent appeal to both the Hindus and the Muslims to understand and appreciate each other's religion, and live in harmony. . . .

THE HINDU, Madras.

. . . For those who wish to be acquainted with the life of the "Prophet of Islam" and the basic principles of Islam without referring to a bigger volume, the book would prove of much use and interest.

THE BOMBAY CHRONICLE, Bombay.

. . . It is for the Muslim students who come from uninspiring homes that books like this are valuable. . . It may do much good among the young men of Western education whom the author had in mind when he wrote it.

THE ISLAMIC CULTURE, Hyderabad (Deccan).

We commend this book heartily to our readers, Muslims as well as non-Muslims. It is a handy life of the Prophet, conceived in a refreshingly liberal and rational spirit. . . . We wish there were lots of true sons of Islam like Maulvi Abdul Karim Sahib in India, for then the Hindu-Muslim problem would be solved in the twinkling of an eye.

THE YOUNG BUILDER, Karachi.

What strikes one about this book is its comprehensiveness, its directness of purpose and the simplicity of its language. . . . The Prophet of Islam should be in the possession of both Christians and Muslims, both of whom may obtain information and inspiration from its pages.

THE COMET, LAGOS, NIGERIA (Africa).